INTERPRETING THE NATIONAL CURRICULUM AT KEY STAGE 1

A developmental approach

EARLY YEARS CURRICULUM GROUP

Open University Press
Buckingham · Philadelphia

This publication has been written by the following members of the Early Years Curriculum Group:

Margaret Edgington (formerly Lally)
Julie Fisher
Michael Morgan
Linda Pound
Wendy Scott

Other members of the group who contributed to this document include:

Geva Blenkin
Vicky Hurst
Jenefer Joseph
Janet Moyles
Elizabeth Sestini
Marian Whitehead

The Early Years Curriculum Group is a nationally recognized body of early years specialists, sharing between them many years' experience of classroom teaching, advising, writing and research about educational management and practice and child development.

At an inaugural meeting with representatives of the Department of Education and Science in October 1988, the group stated its firm beliefs:

1 A distinctive early years curriculum exists in the United Kingdom. It has an established tradition and a fundamental character.
2 This curriculum is dependent on clearly defined goals which are carefully evaluated and assessed.
3 To achieve this, highly trained staff, well versed in child development and clear in their own thinking are necessary.

Their first document, *Early Childhood Education: The Early Years Curriculum and the National Curriculum*, which was published in 1989, focused on the relationship between good practice for children aged 3 to 7 and the National Curriculum. This was followed in 1992 by *First Things First*, which explained the importance of offering the curriculum in a way which is appropriate for young children as they start school. This next book, *Interpreting the National Curriculum at Key Stage 1*, aims to help staff working within Key Stage 1 to establish suitable ways of working with children from 5 to 8 within the context of the statutory requirements.

Open University Press
Celtic Court
22 Ballmoor
Buckingham
MK18 1XW

email: enquiries@openup.co.uk
world wide web: http://www.openup.co.uk

and

325 Chestnut Street
Philadelphia, PA 19106, USA

First Published 1998

A catalogue record of this book is available from the British Library

ISBN 0 335 20175 X

Library of Congress Cataloging-in-Publication Data
Early Years Curriculum Group.
   Interpreting the national curriculum: a developmental approach to Key Stage 1 of the national curriculum/Early Years Curriculum Group
       p. cm.
   Includes bibliographical references (p. 72)
   ISBN 0-335-20175-X
   1. Education, Primary–Great Britain–Curricula.
   2. Curriculum planning–Great Britain. 3. Active learning–Great Britain. 4. Learning, Psychology of. I. Title.
LB1523.E154 1998
2372.19'0941–dc21   97-47476
                                                            CIP

Copy-editing and production coordination by The Running Head Limited, London and Cambridge
Designed and typeset by Marcus Askwith
Printed in Great Britain by St Edmundsbury Press Ltd, Bury St Edmunds, Suffolk

CONTENTS

PREFACE: A DEVELOPMENTALLY APPROPRIATE APPROACH TO THE NATIONAL CURRICULUM

It is some years since the Early Years Curriculum Group first set out a developmental approach to the emerging proposals for a statutory National Curriculum (EYCG 1989). Many changes and reformulations have shaped the National Curriculum since then which have created an urgent need for a new set of developmental guidelines for Key Stage 1 teachers.

We have based our approach on the importance of interpreting the statutory requirements and wish to highlight the complex professional judgements and expertise central to any acts of interpretation. One of the most valuable features of this document is the emphasis it places on the responsibility and professionalism of the Key Stage 1 teacher. A set of national statutory curriculum requirements and a set of developmental guidelines have this at least in common: they are implemented by individual teachers, for good or ill, in terms of children's lives and education.

Interpretation may be a challenging professional responsibility but it is not impossible, and this contribution offers some positive ways forward. At the heart of the document is a detailed analysis of the programmes of study within the National Curriculum. It is written from a learner-centred early years perspective and, as such, does not shrink from pointing out some of the dangers inherent in the current requirements at Key Stage 1 within the National Curriculum. Problematic areas which give us all cause for concern include: the undermining of play; a view of teaching as telling and the simple transference of facts from teacher to taught; the lack of any serious acknowledgement of the importance of learning and its complexity; a consequent preoccupation with subject-centred planning; and a deeply disturbing tendency to assume and promote ethnocentric approaches. Recent pressures to narrow the curriculum are also worrying. Young children are much less likely to see the point of reading, writing and number if they encounter them in a vacuum, unrelated to worthwhile and meaningful content. Too forward an approach imposed too soon risks turning children off learning, and undermines motivation for years to come.

We would not, however, wish to suggest to hard-pressed early years teachers and the families of young children that all is doom and gloom, with no clear path out of the woods. We believe it is possible to prevent the National Curriculum pressurizing teachers and other adults working with young children into wholly inappropriate practices. We hope this document can help early years teachers make a significant act of interpretation: to define continuity in terms of children's experiences, rather than as top-down subject content. We hope, too, it will help parents, practitioners and children understand that valid effort and learning does not necessarily result in tangible outcomes. Like adult scientists, young children can learn from errors and thought-provoking 'mistakes'.

We trust that our developmental approach to the programmes of study will strengthen belief in the power and the potential of young learners and give Key Stage 1 teachers renewed confidence in their interpretations of the National Curriculum. We hope that the forthcoming review of the National Curriculum at Key Stage 1 will take into account the power of young children's thinking, and will result in a more appropriate framework to support and extend their learning, along the lines suggested in this book.

INTRODUCTION

The revised orders for the National Curriculum have presented a host of challenges and opportunities for teachers of young children. However, tensions remain between the principle of an education which starts with the needs and interests of children, and the demands of an externally imposed curriculum. Some teachers have found it difficult to sustain the well-established principles of early childhood education in their practice, and they are expressing concern that they find themselves working in ways which are not effective for young learners.

In Britain, early childhood has traditionally been defined as including children up to the age of 7 or 8. This definition has also been seen as making sound sense in terms of children's development in many European countries, where children start more-formal schooling at a later stage than in the United Kingdom. Our early start to statutory schooling is an accident of history (Moss and Penn 1996). We should not wish to return to a period where, as many of our Victorian school buildings still testify, the youngest children were referred to as the 'babies', and were expected to fit rigid expectations for behaviour. On the contrary, we should take care to safeguard young children's characteristic approaches to learning, since it is these which will make them into lifelong learners. Gardner (1993) emphasizes the importance of the early years of schooling. While acknowledging the role of education in introducing children to the broader culture, he states that 'education should try to preserve the most remarkable features of the young mind – its adventurousness, its generativity, its resourcefulness, and its flashes of flexibility and creativity' (p. 111).

This book supports practitioners in their attempts to address these professional concerns, and offers a developmentally appropriate interpretation of the National Curriculum. Its purpose is to enable teachers of young children to fulfil the legal requirements placed upon them while ensuring that the vital elements necessary to children's long-term development are positively encouraged (Laevers 1994). These include playfulness (Papousek et al. 1992), opportunities for physical activity (Athey 1990) and support for their social and emotional development (Dunn 1988).

A recent publication from the School Curriculum and Assessment Authority (SCAA 1995) has reiterated that the National Curriculum can be taught during the six terms of Years 1 and 2. This is the period when all children in Key Stage 1 are of statutory school age. During the reception year, summer-born children who are not legally required to be at school – and children below statutory school age who are in nursery and reception classes – are intended to have a curriculum which will lead to the achievements described in *Nursery Education: Desirable Outcomes for Children's Learning on Entering Compulsory Education* (SCAA 1996).

Nursery and reception teachers, therefore, have every reason to develop an appropriate curriculum. So long as the areas of experience outlined in the desirable learning outcomes (DLOs) are included, teachers are able to plan appropriately to meet the needs of their children. Teachers who feel that it is essential to include some National Curriculum work at this early stage should focus on the processes included in the National Curriculum rather than be constrained by undertaking content that is not relevant.

This book is aimed primarily at teachers of children in Years 1 and 2. They too may need to take account of the DLOs, because some children 'will require continued support for achieving all or some of the outcomes after entering compulsory education. A small number of children with special educational needs may continue to make progress towards all or some of the outcomes throughout their educational careers' (SCAA 1996: 1).

Teachers at Key Stage 1 should also make sure they claim the 20 per cent of the available curriculum time which is retained for schools' own priorities. Children need time to play, to reflect, to grow and develop; these are, for them, the basics. Teachers must ensure that these legitimate learning needs are met and that all adults working with young children understand how to put into practice important research evidence about early development.

Effective teaching in the early years – the pedagogy of early learning – received the least attention among the views expressed from all quarters when the report of the 'Three Wise Men' (Alexander et al. 1992) provided a catalyst for debate about how the curriculum should be implemented. As Anning (1995: 12) noted, 'The secret garden of the school curriculum has been neatly divided into beds; assessment has been dug, raked and hoed, but pedagogy remains a wilderness.'

Despite all the rhetoric about children needing instruction, and the desirability of having more whole-class teaching, it is essential that early childhood educators hold on to the research evidence which shows the effectiveness of practical, experiential learning; the significance of the social context of learning; the vital role of adult intervention in 'scaffolding' children's learning, and the dangers of introducing them to too formal a curriculum too soon (David *et al.* 1993). There are complexities in working with young children, but teaching in the early years need not be a wilderness. Staff should use their knowledge of child development to understand the individuals in their group, and then *interpret* the programmes of study and offer them in ways that are relevant and meaningful to the children with whom they work.

BACKGROUND

How children learn – underlying principles

In common with our previous publications (EYCG 1989, 1992) the material in this book sprang from the principles of early childhood education. We focused on four non-negotiable aspects which are essential if teachers are to maintain effective early years practice:

- early education must be rooted in children's prior knowledge and experiences;
- young children learn best through being actively and socially involved;
- effective teaching and learning occur in the partnership between young learners and teachers when their ideas and feelings are exchanged, validated and developed;
- if young children are to learn how to participate in a democratic society, they must have opportunities to take responsibility for their actions and intentions.

From these points, we identified vital elements in the learning process which we used in undertaking a systematic examination of each line of each programme of study for every subject. The elements are:

- active learning
- interactive learning
- decision making
- reflecting
- representing.

Challenges for teachers

In developing this document we uncovered a number of significant issues which present challenges for teachers in reconciling the demands of the National Curriculum and children's learning needs. Difficulties are often encountered by teachers in identifying strategies for promoting:

- play
- learning outdoors
- formative assessment
- equal opportunities
- cross-curricular links
- developmental planning.

The appendices indicate where there are good opportunities to promote these elements, as well as danger points.

PLAY
Most infant teachers would acknowledge that young children need opportunities to learn through play, and yet research has shown that their practice does not always reflect this belief (Tizard *et al.* 1988; Bennett and Kell 1989; Bennett and Wood 1997). On inservice courses, it is clear that many early years teachers are not confident in planning for learning through play, and visits to infant classrooms reveal play provision which is poorly resourced and often cramped, if it is there at all. The National Curriculum has not been the cause of this ambivalence, but it has provided an excuse for some teachers ('we haven't got time to let them play now'). On a more positive note, many infant departments are now requesting inservice training on developing the curriculum through play, because they realize that children need the opportunities for consolidation and extension of learning which are offered through meaningful play contexts.

LEARNING OUTDOORS
Children at Key Stage 1 are bundles of physical energy: they need to be given adequate opportunities to move around because their ongoing muscle and bone development demands it. Too often in Key Stage 1 classes, children are required to sit still for long periods of time when they should have ample opportunities to engage in a range of movement activities which will underpin their intellectual as well as their physical growth (Maude 1996). It is totally

consistent, therefore, that the outside area should be thought of as part of the whole learning environment and not just a place where children release surplus energy at playtime. Projects such as Learning Through Landscapes (Titman 1991) highlight the importance of taking the curriculum outdoors as an enrichment of indoor learning experiences.

As young children are now so often physically inhibited by modern society for various reasons (McNeish and Roberts 1995), it is even more vital that their teachers at school consider carefully the links between play, physical development and curriculum experiences. As with other elements, therefore, we examined the National Curriculum to see where scope exists for children to gain access through the programmes of study to play and learn outdoors.

EQUAL OPPORTUNITIES ISSUES

We were concerned that, in their anxiety to cover curriculum content, teachers might lose sight of crucial equal opportunities implications. We have therefore highlighted content within the programmes of study which particularly requires an awareness of these issues.

CROSS-CURRICULAR LINKS

Young children's learning is not compartmentalized into subjects (Bruce 1987; EYCG 1989), and many experiences provide opportunities for cross-curricular learning. We felt that it was important to indicate some of the cross-curricular opportunities and to highlight the importance of planning that takes account of the different developmental needs of the children in the group.

DEVELOPMENTALLY APPROPRIATE PLANNING

Children in the early years will be at different developmental stages (even if they are the same age) and will have a variety of learning styles. It is not appropriate to offer curriculum content to all children in the same way and at the same time. A range of strategies needs to be used to give all children access to the same experiences. We have emphasized the need for planning to cater for the different developmental needs of children in the class or group.

Sections on all of these challenges will be found in the chapter 'Challenges for teachers'.

ASSESSMENT

When examining the programmes of study and assessment orders, we looked for opportunities for formative assessment, which would enable teachers to adapt the curriculum to children's learning needs. There is a danger that assessment will drive the curriculum and that teachers will teach to the test. Government plans for baseline assessment (SCAA 1997) make this more worrying since they may lead schools to focus on the 'value-added' dimension (Tymms 1996), and to rely on simplistic checklists rather than assessment based on observation.

ANALYSIS OF THE PROGRAMMES OF STUDY

We developed a system to enable us to categorize each element of the National Curriculum programmes of study in relation to opportunities for active and interactive learning, and for decision making, reflection and representation. The codes (and their symbols) which evolved are as follows:

- ✓ *Explicit requirement* – this is a clear requirement and can readily be followed.
- oo *Offers opportunities* – the opportunities are implicit in the Orders; they must be drawn out.
- ? *Needs interpretation* – skilled judgement is needed to interpret the Order appropriately; there are risks which must be avoided.
- ! *Danger* – in addressing these requirements, young children's learning needs are likely to be undermined.

Our full analysis of each programme of study is to be found in Appendices 1–10. This analysis was arrived at after considerable debate and cannot be conclusive. Readers may find it helpful to conduct a similar exercise.

UNDERSTANDING AND INTERPRETING THE REQUIREMENTS

Complying with the programmes of study demands a high degree of skill and expertise. We found that many aspects of the programmes of study for young children needed thoughtful interpretation by trained early years teachers who have confidence in their own insight and skills, in order to ensure that they meet children's needs appropriately. Many teachers working in nursery education have shown great ability in dealing with the new demands and ensuring that developments in practice do not inhibit children's learning. Field and Lally (1996) have detailed the wealth of curriculum documents for children from 3 to 5; the report of the Quality in Diversity project (Early Childhood Education Forum 1998) has shown how the views of practitioners working with children from birth to 8 suggest appropriate interpretations for the 5- to 8-year-olds. Key Stage 1 teachers need to build on effective practice with under-fives, and develop a similarly distinctive approach. This book helps teachers to undertake that interpretation, while developing their own practice and explaining it to others.

We found very few statements which require the category 'danger'. However, there are elements where a higher degree of professional responsibility is required. There is a particular phrase which occurs in a number of sections of the Orders: 'pupils should be taught to . . .' This phrase all too readily suggests a transmission model of practice which needs interpretation in the early years. Young children do not learn effectively if they are merely instructed (Holt 1989). Like all learners, they need opportunities to explore materials, ideas and relationships. As very young learners, they are deluged with new information and experiences. They need to link what is new with their existing knowledge and understanding, so that they can make sense of what they are learning (Sotto 1994).

IMPLICATIONS FOR PRACTICE

Skilled educators will be aware that effective teaching in the early years must include the following strategies:

- observing and analysing learning;
- planning, organizing and managing a richly resourced learning environment;
- listening, responding and asking open-ended questions;
- facilitating, supporting and intervening;
- challenging and posing problems to solve;
- enthusing and building on children's intrinsic motivation;
- collaborating in activities initiated by children;
- reflecting and evaluating.

Young children learn most effectively within an environment (both indoors and outdoors) which offers them the opportunity to make choices, take responsibility, represent their ideas, solve problems and interact with a wide range of materials and people (Bruce 1987; Ofsted 1994; Blenkin and Kelly 1996; SCAA 1996; Edgington 1998).

In the next chapter we have taken each element of the learning process in turn and explained what we mean by active and interactive learning, where children come to responsible decisions, reflect upon their learning and represent their own ideas. We have then highlighted key words and phrases from the National Curriculum which are compatible with this way of working, presented them in diagrams as well as in the text, and have provided examples of what they mean in practice.

VITAL ELEMENTS WITHIN THE LEARNING PROCESS

ACTIVE LEARNING

There is a growing body of research evidence which indicates that young children need to be active learners and not passive recipients of a curriculum (David *et al.* 1993). From birth, children actively explore their surroundings. Their intellectual development depends on physical experience. This interaction (based on EYCG 1989; Lally 1995) includes:

- sensory exploration (touching, observing, listening, mouthing and smelling);
- imitating;
- discussing and questioning;
- making connections;
- problem solving.

For young children much is new and puzzling. If they are to learn effectively, they need first-hand experience of objects, materials, people and situations, and they need to talk about these experiences in order to consolidate their learning. Katz and Chard (1989: 22) stress that:

> young children's knowledge is mainly behavioural and is strongly embedded in the context in which it was learned. Three-year-olds may possess the behavioural knowledge to navigate through rooms of their own home and perhaps their immediate neighbourhood. But they probably cannot represent this knowledge abstractly in the form of a sketch or map.

They go on to argue that children need a rich store of experiences to build up their behavioural knowledge and understanding of the world and to provide a firm basis for acquiring abstract representational knowledge. When observing young children in nursery and infant settings it is clear that they need opportunities to behave as readers and writers, scientists, mathematicians and so on, representing their ideas in their own way as a foundation for the introduction to more formal ways of recording words, numbers and ideas. Through experimenting in the water tray, for example, children will discover that some things float and some things sink to the bottom of the tray.

This investigation is a form of scientific behaviour through which knowledge is developed. Children may be encouraged to represent their findings, or may do so spontaneously through talk, through grouping objects, or by drawing them.

First-hand experience is vital if children are eventually to make sense of abstract representation, and yet too often teachers start from, or introduce too early, ways of working which are not connected to practical experience. For example, a group of Year 1 children had been given a geography work sheet on which they had been asked to draw places and things which were near their home, far away from their home and very far away from their home. It was clear that many of the children had little understanding of relative distance. Asking children to work in an abstract, passive way of this kind before they have developed conceptual understanding through a wide range of relevant experience is to cut them off from learning.

Key words and phrases from the programmes of study (see p. 6)

An informed analysis of the National Curriculum (DES 1989) shows that children should be taught in ways which encourage them to be active. Most of the sections within the programmes of study demand that children engage in the processes outlined above if they are to be able to learn. Even where the programmes of study appear to demand active experiences, teachers may interpret this in ways which can result in passive or relatively alienating learning for children. For example, in the art curriculum (7c), children are required not only to use two- and three-dimensional media but to explore them. Teachers often place too much emphasis on use and do not allow sufficient time and focus for active exploration. When interpreting the programmes of study, teachers should ask themselves whether they are enabling children to engage in active learning processes. Are children able to think and do things for themselves? In (experimental and investigative) science (2a), do children have opportunities actively to 'explore using appropriate senses', or in English (speaking and listening) (1a), are children actively encouraged to play

English

Speaking and listening

Talk for a range of purposes:

1a • Telling stories, both real and imagined; imaginative play and drama; reading and listening to nursery rhymes and poetry; learning some by heart; reading aloud

• Exploring, developing and clarifying ideas; predicting outcomes and discussing possibilities

• Describing events, observations and experiences; making simple, clear explanations of choices; giving reasons for opinions and actions

3b Extend vocabulary through activities that encourage interest in words, including exploration and discussions of: words with similar and opposite meanings, word games, words associated with specific occasions

Reading

1a Have extensive experience of children's literature. Pupils should read on their own, with others and to the teacher, from a range of genres that includes stories, poetry, plays and picture books. Pupils should read their own writing to the teacher and others

2d Use reference materials for different purposes. They should be taught about the structural devices for organizing information, e.g. contents, headings, captions

Writing

1b Write in response to a variety of stimuli, including stories, poems, classroom activities and personal experience. Pupils should be taught to identify the purpose for which they write and to write for a range of readers, e.g. their teacher, their family, their peers, themselves

2b Plan and review their writing, assembling and developing their ideas on paper and on screen

Mathematics

Using and applying mathematics

1a Use and apply mathematics in practical tasks, in real-life problems and within mathematics itself

Number

1a Develop flexible methods of working with number, orally and mentally

5a Sort and classify a set of objects using criteria related to their properties, e.g. size, shape, mass

Shape, space and measures

1a Gain a wide range of practical experience using a variety of materials

2b Make common 3-D and 2-D shapes and models

Science

General requirements

1a Ask questions, e.g. how? why? what will happen?

1b Use focused exploration and investigation to acquire scientific knowledge, understanding and skills

Experimental and investigative science

2a Obtain evidence to explore using appropriate senses

2b Make observations and measurements

2c Make a record of observations and measurements

Materials and their properties

1a Use senses to explore and recognize the similarities and differences between materials

2a Objects made from some materials can be changed in shape by processes including squashing, bending, twisting and stretching

Design and technology

1a Design and make products

1c Investigate, disassemble and evaluate simple products

4a Select materials, tools and techniques

4b Measure, mark out, cut and shape a range of materials

ACTIVE LEARNING

Geography

1a Investigate the physical and human features of their surroundings

2 In investigating places and a theme, question and record, communicate ideas and information

3b Undertake fieldwork activities in the locality of the school, e.g. observing housing types, mapping the school playground

Information technology

1a Use a variety of IT equipment and software, including microcomputers and various keyboards, to carry out a variety of functions in a range of contexts

3b Give direct signals or commands that produce a variety of outcomes, and describe the effects of their actions

History

1a Investigate changes in their own lives and those of their family or adults around them

1b Investigate aspects of the way of life of people in Britain in the past beyond living memory

Physical education

1c Engage in activities that develop cardiovascular health, flexibility, muscular strength and endurance

3e Warm up for and recover from exercise

Areas of activity

1b (Games) Develop and practise a variety of ways of sending (including throwing, striking, rolling and bouncing), receiving and travelling with a ball and other similar games equipment

Music

1a Use sounds and respond to music individually, in pairs, in groups and as a class

4a Control sounds made

4b Perform with others and develop an awareness of audience, venue and occasion

5e Improvise musical patterns

6d Respond to musical elements

Art

1 Experience different approaches to art, craft and design, including those that involve working individually, in groups and as a whole class

7b Gather resources and materials, using them to stimulate and develop ideas

7c Explore and use 2 and 3 dimensional media, working on a variety of scales

8d Experiment with tools and techniques for drawing, painting, printmaking, collage and sculpture, exploring a range of materials including textiles

imaginatively? History and geography frequently pose difficulties for teachers in providing active experiences. However history (1a) can be more actively interpreted if the investigative aspects are stressed through, for example, drawing on changes over time by inviting in family members from different generations. Similarly, geography (2) could involve children in taking photographs to generate a display of their environmental experiences.

Other parts of the programmes of study appear to be less supportive of active learning. For example, art (section 4 of the programme of study for Key Stage 1) requires that:

> Throughout their work, children should be taught about visual, and where appropriate, tactile elements, including:
>
> (a) pattern and texture in natural and man-made forms;
> (b) colour matching and how colour is mixed from primary colours;
> (c) how images are made using line and tone;
> (d) the use of shape, form and space in images and artefacts.

From this, teachers may assume that art should be approached through demonstration and instruction. Children need to engage in art activities which promote both exploration of and discussion about cause and effect. This will enable them to come to an understanding of their own which will expand their mathematical and scientific knowledge as well as their aesthetic appreciation.

Examples of active learning in practice

Contrast the different learning experiences of two Year 1 classes: both are focusing on sunflowers for art 'appreciation' and 'representation' purposes. In one class, the teacher provided a postcard of Van Gogh's sunflowers, paper and ready-mixed paints. In the other class children had ample opportunities before recording to handle, describe, observe through hand lenses and generally to investigate the form of the plant both in flower and seed (they even fed the birds with them).

Not only was this active experience vital for children's motivation and learning, it also promoted better outcomes and provided a context for children to increase their independence.

A visit to a real baker's shop could be used as the basis for a wide range of active learning opportunities within the programmes of study. If it is not possible for the teacher to take groups on an outing of this sort, parents could be encouraged to make a focused visit to a baker's shop at the weekend. The creation of a bakery in the classroom could lead to:

- designing and building the shop;
- children making some real food (for example, pitta or soda bread, chapatis, and cakes);
- selling and buying activities;
- making longer-lasting props from dough.

INTERACTIVE LEARNING

Research evidence consistently shows the importance of young children being directly and actively involved in first-hand experiential learning. It also shows how this leads to the development of their conceptual understanding (Vygotsky 1978; Wells 1987; Athey 1990). The transmission model of learning which characterizes children as empty vessels waiting to be filled – having 'knowledge squirted at them' (Holt 1989: 148–9) – is incomplete. The contrasting Piagetian view that children are somehow preprogrammed to develop through a series of stages does not give sufficient emphasis to the role of other people in children's learning.

Whatever their personal and social circumstances, young children come to school with many skills and with a host of knowledge culled from their experience, which will expand and flourish in a stimulating context. Drawing on their knowledge of how children learn, teachers are responsible for providing a supportive structure to 'scaffold' learning for the children. The chosen path through the curriculum is formed through awareness of what children already know and would like to learn more about, and what they need to know next. For learning to be effective, children need opportunities for:

- interaction with the teacher, which includes higher-order discussion and negotiated learning;
- interaction with other children, learning to collaborate and to apply knowledge and skills to solving problems.

There are, of course, pragmatic issues to be resolved in the implementation of this approach to learning. *The scope of the National Curriculum places great demands on teachers if the programmes of study are to be interpreted in a way which facilitates effective early learning.* We know from classroom-based research the importance of high levels of questioning from the teacher (Rowlands 1984; Brown and Wragg 1993) and of the need to adopt strategies which allow maximum levels of sustained interaction with all children. Yet often young children work independently even when they are arranged in groups, with the teacher having to scurry between them, trying to give individual attention to all. The result is low-level interaction, with little use made of the potential for collaboration (Galton and Williamson 1992). There is evidence that when teachers take individual children as their main focus, many of their interactions are routine, organizational and low level. The children may receive little teacher attention, working mostly on their own; extended discussions, including higher-order questions, may be severely limited. In order to achieve sustained interaction, much more needs to be made of collaborative group work (Chang and Wells 1988; Hastings and Schwieso 1995). Bruner (1977: 8) points out that:

> so much of learning depends upon the need to achieve joint attention, to conduct enterprises jointly, to honour the social relationships that exist . . . to generate possible worlds in which propositions may be true or appropriate, or even felicitous; to overlook this functional setting of learning whatever its content, is to dry it to a mummy.

Young children need to be helped to bridge the gap which exists between what they can do alone and what they can do with support through cooperative activity set in an appropriate context (Vygotsky 1978). By fostering the development of independence, establishing clear routines and expectations for behaviour in the classroom, and engaging children in self- and peer-assessment related to worthwhile activities, teachers can release themselves to work with individuals and small groups. It is generally more effective to use classroom assistants for management tasks so that teachers can focus directly on children's learning (Moyles 1997).

Key words and phrases from the programmes of study (see p. 9)

Examination of the programmes of study for most areas of the National Curriculum will show that there are aspects which require interaction if they are to make any sense to the learner: for example, imaginative play and drama, giving reasons for opinions and actions in English or asking the questions 'What will happen if . . .?' in science.

There are also many places where an *interpretation* by the teacher can provide an organization for learning which maximizes sustained teacher intervention and effective collaborative learning. The scope of activity required for the investigations and problem solving in design and technology and scientific enquiry provide many opportunities for cooperation and interaction with others which result in more-rigorous procedures and more-imaginative solutions. There are many instances where play will provide the liveliest and most meaningful context. As the Brunerian and Vygotskian approaches suggest, the younger the children, the more they learn from spoken language and the less from text. The programmes of study for English include the following activities to which children should have access:

- telling stories;
- exploring, developing and clarifying ideas;
- working in groups of different sizes;
- listening to others' reactions;
- participation in drama activities, improvisation and performance;
- taking turns in speaking and the conventions of discussion and conversation.

Hall and Robinson (1995) highlight the importance of socio-dramatic play in providing a context within which children quickly learn to cooperate, as the example below illustrates. Fisher (1996: 87) points out: 'children will not co-operate simply because it is in the teacher's plans. Yet young children will co-operate and collaborate with commitment when they see the need to do so.'

Examples of interactive learning in practice

A group of 6-year-olds had been investigating how the insertion of various materials into a simple circuit (battery, wire, bulb) either interrupted the flow of electricity or allowed it to continue. Having come to some agreement as to which combination of materials conducted electricity best (all metal), the teacher asked how they might use one or more of the objects as a switch. This was duly investigated. When the children had sorted out their ideas, the teacher asked if they could devise a way of demonstrating to the whole class what they had done. The children came up with the solution of using themselves as the battery, the bulb and, by joining hands and forming a circle, the wire. By breaking hands at one point and pivoting smartly on his heel, one boy demonstrated how he,

English

Speaking and listening

1a • Explore, develop, clarify ideas; predict outcomes; discuss possibilities
 • Describe events; make simple, clear explanations
 • Give reasons for opinions
1b Consider how talk is influenced by purpose and audience
2a • Speak with confidence, organizing what they say
 • Choose words with precision, taking into account the needs of the listeners
 • Take turns in speaking
2b • Listen with growing attention; respond appropriately and effectively
 • Develop thinking and extend ideas in the light of discussion
 • Take different views into account

Reading

1a • Read on their own or with others, from a range of genres
 • Read their own writing to the teacher and others
1b Make use of a range of sources of information
1c Use materials read and discussed to stimulate pupils' imagination and enthusiasm
2c • Talk about characters and events; begin to use appropriate terminology
 • Explain the content of a passage or whole text
 • Choose books with others
 • Review reading with their teacher

Writing

1b • Write in response to a variety of stimuli
 • Identify the purpose of writing and write for a range of readers
1c Present writing in different ways helpful to purpose, task and reader
2a Differentiate between print and pictures; undertake connections between speech and writing
2b • Have opportunities to plan and review their writing
 • Collaborate and read work aloud
3a Discuss the organization of more complex texts
3b Develop interest in words through consideration and discussion

Mathematics

Using and applying mathematics

1b Explain their thinking to support the development of their reasoning
3c/4b Discuss work, respond to and ask mathematical questions: why? what would happen if?

Shape, size and measures

3a Describe positions, copy, continue and make patterns

Science

General requirements

1a Ask questions – how? why? what will happen?
1b Use focused explanation and investigation
2a Relate to domestic/environmental contexts

Experimental and investigative science

2a Explore using appropriate senses
3a Communicate what happened during their work
3e Indicate evidence supporting predictions
3f Explain what they found out

Life processes and living things

1b Animals including humans, move, feed, grow, use their senses and reproduce
4c Recognize similarity and difference

Design and technology

1c Investigate and disassemble simple products
3b Clarify ideas through discussion
3e/4c Suggest how to proceed (with an enquiry)
3f Consider design ideas, identify strengths and weaknesses

Geography

2 Investigate places and themes; observe, question and learn; communicate ideas and information
6a Express views about attractive and unattractive features of environments

INTERACTIVE LEARNING

Information technology

1c Examine and discuss experience of IT
2a Generate and communicate ideas in text, pictures, etc.
2c Use IT-based models/ simulations to explore aspects of real/imaginary situations

History

1a Investigate changes in their own lives and those of their family or adults around them

Physical education

1a Be physically active
1c Engage in activities to develop cardiovascular health, flexibility, strength and endurance
2a Observe the conventions of fair play, honest competition and good sporting behaviour as individual team members and spectators
3d Lift, carry, place and use equipment safely

Areas of activity

1a (Games) Play simple and competitive games

Dance

3c Explore moods and feelings through dance

Music

1a Use sounds and respond to music individually and in groups
3a Include music from different times and cultures
4b Perform with others
4d Communicate musical ideas
4f Respond to and evaluate live performances and recorded music
5c Sing unison songs
5d Share music making
5f Explore, create, select and organize sounds in simple structures
5g Use sounds to create musical effects
5h Record compositions

Art

8f Review work they have done and describe what they might change or develop in future work
9e Describe works of art, craft and design in simple terms, and explain what they think and feel about these

the switch, could turn the bulb on or off. The bulb child waggled her head vigorously to indicate 'on'. The children faced the direction of the current and thus made their explanation so clear that 'being a circuit' became a playtime game for a number of groups.

Some 5-year-olds wanted to create a garage play setting. The teacher was reluctant, expecting such play to favour boys, to be short-lived and to lead to little productive learning. The children persisted, and the teacher (half-hoping to dissuade them) told them that in order to build a garage they would need 'planning permission'. The inevitable question resulted in the teacher scribing a letter on the children's behalf to the planning department and the subsequent return of a genuine planning permission form. This was duly completed including such items as 'three strides wide and 25 hands high' in the 'proposed dimensions' section. The notion became a whole-class concern with subsequent advertisements being composed for staff at the garage, interviews being held, jobs being given. The placing of clear instructions by customers for a service were required, with all the resulting talk and development of ideas. Plentiful opportunities for real collaborative learning were taking place; the children were engrossed and able to make relevant decisions within a framework maintained and enriched by the teacher. She gave sustained time to the development of ideas, and posed questions which challenged the children's thinking.

DECISION MAKING

Learning requires children to accommodate new experiences and understandings into their developing framework of the world (Athey 1990). The more opportunities children have to exercise choice and make decisions, the greater the possibility that they will be in control of the learning experience and make sense of it.

When children make decisions it is necessary that they understand the purpose of the task in hand, otherwise they have no criteria by which to make that decision. Decision making by children requires the teacher to hand over control. If children are to have genuine choices they cannot be constrained in their decisions by the teacher (Warham 1993). Teachers who prescribe what is to be taught, when, with whom, and for how long, leave children with no decisions to make and no control over their learning environment. The range of possibilities offered, such as which resources to use, or which investigation to pursue,

should be sufficiently broad to ensure that the element of choice is meaningful. This exercise of control is a motivating and liberating force for children as learners, and encourages them to become responsible and autonomous.

The classroom environment needs to be organized and managed in ways which facilitate independent work. Decisions about the use of space and resources can all be shared with children who are capable, with appropriate initial support, to make choices about what resources and materials to use, where to locate them, how to use them and where they should be returned (Moyles 1992; Fisher 1996). When children make decisions they become active participants in the business of learning. Knowledge is not transmitted directly from the teacher to the learner; learners must engage in the activity in order to understand the choices they have, and thus be able to make appropriate decisions (Rowlands 1984).

Children are most likely to be in control of a learning situation when they play. Play is the means by which children can be in control, by using the technical prowess, mastery and competence they have previously developed (Bruce 1991, 1996). Play enables children to make decisions about what they do, who they are, who they become, who they are with and what they experience (Moyles 1989). It gives children control over resources and materials to use with imagination and creativity (Gura 1992). These choices are motivating. Being in control of learning experiences also raises children's self-esteem (Roberts 1995) and gives them a greater sense of responsibility over the outcome of their actions (Hohmann and Weikart 1995).

Key words and phrases in the programmes of study (see p. 11)

Many of the statements within the programmes of study explicitly require children to make decisions. They are required to select appropriate resources and choose from a range of materials. Children are expected to make choices about the content of their work and the processes which they use. They have to make decisions about how to record and present their ideas. They are required to give clear explanations for the choices they have made.

Design and technology provides excellent possibilities for decision making; mathematics is also good and there is a lot of potential in science and art. Other subjects present few explicit opportunities.

English

Speaking and listening

1a • Explore, develop and clarify ideas; predict outcomes and discuss possibilities
   • Describe events, observations and experiences; make simple, clear explanations of choices, giving reasons for opinions and actions
1d Participate in improvisation
2a Communicate effectively to a range of audiences
2b Respond effectively to what they have heard, and ask and answer questions that clarify understanding

Reading

2a Use various approaches to word identification and recognition
2b Confirm the sense of what has been read
2d Use reference materials for different purposes

Writing

1b Write in response to a variety of stimuli
2b • Plan and review writing
   • Make choices about vocabulary

Mathematics

Using and applying mathematics

2a Select and use appropriate maths
2b Select and use mathematical equipment and materials
2c Look for ways to overcome (mathematical) difficulties

Number

1a Develop flexible methods of work with number
4a/b Use number operations to solve problems
4c Choose a suitable method of computation
5a Sort and classify a set of objects
5b Interpret data

Shape, space and measures

2b Classify shapes
4a Compare objects and events using appropriate language
4b Choose and use simple measuring instruments

Science

Experimental and investigative science

1a Turn ideas into a form that can be investigated
1b Think about what is expected to happen when planning
3c Make simple comparisons
3d Use results to draw conclusions
3f Try to explain what they have found

Materials and their properties

1b/e Sort materials into groups and select for different purposes

Design and technology

1a Design products
2b Investigate how the work characteristics of materials can be changed to suit different purposes
2c Apply skills, knowledge and understanding from the PoS of other subjects
3a Draw on own experience to help generate ideas
3c Shaping/assembling/ rearranging
3d Develop and communicate design ideas
3e/4e Make suggestions about how to proceed
3f Consider design ideas
4a Select materials, tools and techniques
4f Evaluate products

Geography

6c Express views on the attractive and unattractive features of environments

DECISION MAKING

Information technology

3b Give commands that produce a variety of outcomes

History

Key elements

1a Sequence events and objects
2c Identify differences between ways of life at different times
4b Ask and answer questions about the past

Physical education

1b Adopt the best possible posture
2a Observe the conventions of fair play, honest competition and good sporting behaviour
3b Recognize and follow relevant rules, laws, codes, etiquette and safety procedures

Music

4c Compose in response to a variety of stimuli
4f Respond to and evaluate live performances and recorded music
5e Improvise musical patterns
5f Explore, create, select and organize sounds in simple structures

Art

2c Design and make images and artefacts
7d/8f Review and modify work
7f Respond to and evaluate art, craft and design
8c Select and sort images and artefacts
8d Experiment with tools and techniques
8e Experiment with visual elements
9c Recognize differences and similarities in art, craft and design
9e Describe works of art, craft and design and explain what they think and feel about these

Examples of decision making in practice

A group of 7-year-old children was planning to write a book for children in a younger class. The older children talked to the younger ones in order to find out what kind of stories they liked and which characters they enjoyed. They found out which formats were popular and whether illustrations were appreciated. They then used all this information to write a story with their audience in mind, making decisions about the text and its illustrations.

This apparently simple everyday example is capable of yielding a rich interpretation. At one level, the full range of the National Curriculum English requirements can be met in this activity. Clearly the children involved are speaking and listening in purposeful ways which are sensitive to their audience (younger and older peers) based on making and modifying a sequence of decisions. This activity built on previous experiences with books of many kinds (pop-ups, pictures, flaps, etc.) and on an awareness of the range and subtlety of book language. Obviously the children were seeing themselves as responsible readers, writers and authors. There are other levels of interpretation which indicate the presence in this example of all the vital elements of the learning process discussed earlier.

Another primary school decided to develop its outdoor learning environment. Each class brainstormed with the teacher what they wanted. The Year 1 class asked for a quiet area where they could play without being disturbed by older children's games, some climbing equipment and toys for outdoor play. They volunteered their parents' help with tasks.

Early stages of the work would meet many requirements of the English programmes of study, including 'exploring, developing and clarifying ideas; predicting outcomes and discussing possibilities . . . giving reasons for opinions and actions' while working with the teacher to develop plans for all aspects of the environment.

Gathering evidence for decision making would involve children in explorations, including geographical skills of investigation, mapping and expressing views on how the environment can be improved. Mathematics would be applied in the real-life context and children would need to explain their thinking and reasoning. They would use mathematics to make and monitor their decisions and to ask questions about the outcomes of their actions.

In refining their enquiries children would have an opportunity to use 'focused exploration and investigation' to acquire knowledge and understanding of the scientific implications of their proposals and consider 'how to treat living things and the environment with sensitivity'. Scientific skills of obtaining and considering evidence would be involved. In planning the development of the area, children would be encouraged to think about what is expected to happen and to understand that this is useful when planning what to do; they would also be taught how to turn ideas into a form that can be investigated.

Design of the environment would enable children to develop and practise particular skills and knowledge of design and technology in focused practical tasks. In dealing with these tasks they would be able to use a variety of IT equipment and software to generate and communicate their ideas in different forms; they would be able to use IT-based models or simulations to explore aspects of real and imaginary situations. At this point, in order to develop visual literacy, children could be taught about the different ways in which ideas, feelings and meanings are communicated in visual form and could be helped to explore ways of representing what they would like to see in their environment. If there were any craftspeople or artists among their parents, this would be an opportunity to be introduced to what was involved in their work and how they, the children, could participate or help.

In recording the development of the plans, children would come to understand the value of writing as a means of remembering, communicating, organizing and developing ideas and information. Although the opportunities for history did not seem plentiful, the written record, made into a book and supplemented by photographs, would enable children to become aware of the changes in the lives and environment of themselves, their parents and the adults at school. The photographs themselves could also be a second way of recording, as a game in which children could try to work out the chronology of events and discuss their reasons for thinking so.

REFLECTING

When we encounter new experiences or ideas as adults, we may become aware of the need to consider how these fit into our existing understanding. Often we must adjust our view in order to take into account any additional information. This process is very individual, and depends on past experience, current interests, and other factors to do with attention, ability and style of learning. There is a personal dimension beyond our own characteristics too: we all know how difficult it is to deal constructively with an unwanted or irrelevant demand on our attention. This human insight is all too often forgotten when we consider how young children learn, although there is evidence that endorses our own personal perceptions about the crucial part that any learner must play in the educational process. It is not enough to be provided with rich experiences and clear explanations about worthwhile content. We all need time to reflect on how these relate to our current level of understanding, and to readjust our perspectives accordingly.

This dimension deserves respect, and must have attention, especially in relation to young children, who are relatively inexperienced learners. It is reciprocated by the complementary requirement that adults working in the early years of education should not be afraid to be seen to be pausing and considering whether an intervention is necessarily desirable when there is no apparent active learning going on. Decisions must be made in the light of knowledge of individual children, together with an awareness of their changing, multifaceted abilities to absorb and transform experience into working hypotheses for living. Claxton (1997: 44–5) points out that:

> As they develop, the range and complexity of the scenarios in which children take part start to expand dramatically . . . They take part in new social groups of various sizes and compositions. They start to meet many different *kinds* of things to be learnt about, and to discover new ways of going about learning them . . . they need to develop a new form of learning, one which enables them to *ruminate* over their experience; to bring back, as the cow does, what has been separately ingested, and by chewing it over make it more homogeneous. They would have to be concerned not just to meet new challenges one by one, but to look actively for points of segmentation and integration.

Wood (1988) highlights the fact that if the young child is to become a truly effective thinker and learner, he needs to be able 'to lift himself out of immediate happenings, to weigh up possibilities, plan his actions

and evaluate his efforts'. In doing this, 'the child is enjoined to decentre, think about and reflect upon his own activities and, in consequence, becomes more analytic, less impulsive and achieves more effective control of his own learning' (p. 143).

Key words and phrases from the programmes of study (see p. 14)

The National Curriculum at Key Stage 1 makes some acknowledgement of the importance of the processes of learning. The requirement for pupils to reflect on their experience, both in and out of school, permeates the documents. It is particularly strong in science and technology, but 'understanding', 'selecting' and 'evaluating' are frequent phrases across all subjects.

In science, the explicit links to first-hand experience throughout require pupils to reflect on their personal knowledge. There is an important strand which deals with the processes of scientific investigation, and the development of scientific skills: experimental science should involve occasions when 'the whole process of investigating an idea should be carried out by pupils themselves'. Planning work and considering evidence expiicitly requires reflection. All the other strands of science should be undertaken in this same spirit of enquiry and problem solving.

Similarly, in technology, pupils should:

- undertake activities in which they investigate . . . and evaluate simple projects;
- investigate how the working characteristics of materials can be changed to suit different purposes;
- draw on their own experience;
- develop their ideas.

There are many examples throughout the strands of technology which require planning based on evaluation or judgement. In practice this means that a wide range of materials should be available that can be used flexibly for different purposes. Pupils should be allowed time to develop their ideas, especially through play, when they can take control of their experiments. Setting aside a place to keep ongoing work encourages the idea that improvements can be made over time.

Parents as well as children and teachers need to understand that valid effort may not necessarily result in tangible outcomes.

Explicit links with past experience, and out-of-school

English

Speaking and listening

1a Explore, develop and classify ideas; predict outcomes and discuss possibilities. Make simple, clear explanations of choices; give reasons for opinions and actions

1c In considering what has been heard, remember specific points that interested them, and listen to others' reactions

2a Make themselves clear through organizing what they say and choosing words with precision. Incorporate relevant detail and distinguish between the essential and the less important, taking into account the needs of their listeners

2b Respond appropriately, clarify their understanding and indicate thoughtfulness about the matter under discussion. Use talk to develop their thinking and extend their ideas in the light of discussion, taking different views into account

3b Extend vocabulary through activities including exploration and interpretation in different contexts

Reading

2a Read with understanding, building on what they already know. Use various approaches to word identification and recognition, and use their understanding of grammatical structure and the meaning of the text as a whole to make sense of print

2b Check the accuracy of their reading, attending to whether it sounds right and/or makes sense grammatically. They should be taught contextual understanding, focusing on meaning

3 Consider the characteristics and features of different kinds of texts

Writing

2b Plan and review their writing, develop their ideas. Make choices about vocabulary and organize imaginative and factual writing

3b Develop interest in words and their meanings, and extend vocabulary through consideration and discussion
. . .

Mathematics

Using and applying mathematics

2a Select the appropriate mathematics

2c Develop different mathematical approaches and look for ways to overcome difficulties

3c Discuss their work, responding to and asking mathematical questions

4a Recognize patterns and relationships and make related predictions about them

Number

3b Explore patterns, explaining their patterns and using them to make predictions; progress to exploring further patterns

4a Understand x and ÷/ relationship between them/ use them to solve problems

4b–d Understand, choose, begin to check answers in different ways

5a Sort and class a set of objects using criteria related to their properties

5b Collect, record and interpret data arising from an area of interest

Science

General requirements

1a Ask questions – how? why? what will happen?

1b Use focused exploration and investigation to acquire scientific understanding

Experimental and investigative science

1b Thinking about what is expected to happen can be useful

1c Recognize when a test or comparison is unfair

3c Consider evidence – make simple comparisons

3f Explain . . . drawing on evidence and conclusions

Life processes and living things

4b Living things can be grouped according to similarities and differences

Design and technology

1c Investigate and evaluate simple projects

2c Apply skills/knowledge of understanding from other subjects

3a Draw on experience to generate ideas

3b Clarify ideas

3c Develop ideas

3e Make suggestions about how to proceed

3f Consider design ideas as they develop and identify strengths and weaknesses

4f Evaluate products

5d Relate the way things work to their intended purpose

Geography

1a Investigate

1b Undertake studies [which] should involve the development of knowledge and understanding

2 In investigating places, observe, question and communicate ideas

5b/c How localities may be similar and how they may be different; the effects of weather

6a Express views on attractive and unattractive features of environments

6b How pupils' environment is changing

6c How the quality of the environment can be sustained and improved

REFLECTING

Information technology

1c Examine and discuss pupils' experiences of IT, and look at the use of IT in the outside world

3a Recognize that control is integral to many everyday devices

History

1a/b Investigate changes in their own lives, and aspects of others' lives

Key elements

2b Recognize why

2c Identify differences

3 Interpret history

4a How to find out

4b Ask and answer questions

Physical education

2b How to cope with success and limitations in performance
Be mindful of others and the environment

Dance

3c Explore moods and feelings and develop their response to music

Music

2a–f When performing, composing, listening and appraising, listen with concentration, internalizing e.g. hearing in their heads and recognizing the musical elements

3 The repertoire [should] develop their appreciation of the richness of our diverse cultural heritage

4e Develop understanding of music from different times and places

4f Evaluate music

5g Use sounds to create musical effects

Art

6 Use materials, tools and techniques for practical work safely

7d Review and modify their work as it progresses

8a Record what has been experienced, observed and imagined

8f Review what they have done and describe what they might change or develop in future work

9c Recognize differences and similarities in art, craft and design from different times and places

contexts, are made in mathematics, and there is a clear requirement that pupils should have more than rote learning. The National Curriculum requires them to:

- understand the language of number, properties of shape and comparatives . . . developing reasoning;
- select . . . [and] check their work;
- develop different approaches;
- explain their thinking to support the development of their reasoning . . . in relation to all other strands of the maths curriculum.

In practice this means that adults must become aware of the processes children engage in as their mathematical understanding grows, and ensure that they are given opportunities to reflect on their work and articulate their thinking as they apply their skills and knowledge.

The role of language in promoting reflection is vital in conceptual development, and should be highlighted, especially in relation to children whose first language is not English. These pupils, together with any who have special educational needs, particularly depend on good links between home and community and their school. It is essential that teachers are conscious of children's existing knowledge and skills, so that they can respond to their suggestions, thus reinforcing rather than preventing reflective thought.

Adults provide very important models for reflective learning. It is essential that they show respect for individual and cultural difference, recognize varying forms of representation, and seek to understand the meanings children are trying to express. The importance of accepting any errors as a constructive part of a reflective learning process must be remembered. 'Wrong' ideas can be very productive in a climate that encourages children to work for intellectual rather than social rewards. This leads to intrinsic motivation, which, as Katz and MacLellan (1991) point out, develops a disposition to work independently and to overcome difficulties.

Examples of reflecting in practice

The mother of a young Year 1 child, having seen other children with gloves on elastic through the sleeves of their coats, decides her child needs a similar device. Unfortunately, she has only a fairly short piece of string. When it comes to going out to play in the morning, the teacher witnesses the following scene:

Kieren puts on his anorak. He gets one glove on to his right hand but the other glove disappears up the left sleeve! He takes off the right glove, retrieves the left glove and puts it on his hand. By this time the right glove has disappeared up the opposite sleeve. He tries twice more to get on both gloves but to no avail. He removes his coat and endeavours to see whether he fares any better in getting on his gloves with the coat upside down. The hood now flaps between his legs like a tail and he has no greater success in getting on the gloves. After some time, he carefully pulls both gloves and string right through one sleeve of his anorak, puts on the coat, hooks the string over his neck and puts on both gloves.

Kieren has clearly reflected in a very serious way on the problem that he encountered and found his own solution through a process of trial and error. The teacher wisely stood back and allowed Kieren time for his learning experience.

The teacher of a Year 1 class has been reading them a story about a haunted house. The children get very excited and begin to think of the kinds of noises which are associated with the experience. The teacher suggests that they choose some musical instruments and make up their own story with sound effects. The children think of all the various things which might appear within the house (skeletons and ghosts are popular) and the atmosphere in different parts of the house (cellar and attic are especially scary), and choose musical sounds to represent them.

REPRESENTING

Representation is a vital part of all learning and goes far beyond recording events, feelings and ideas. In order to think about anything we must represent it in some form. The act of recording causes us to reformulate our ideas, and to infuse that which we have seen, heard or experienced with our prior experiences. The very act of speaking our thoughts out loud or writing something down reshapes our understanding (Gardner 1993). In our society the most commonly used form of representation is either spoken or written language. All children need extensive opportunities to think out loud in the language in which they are most competent and comfortable. If we deny them this opportunity we deny them the right to learn to think for themselves.

There are many other ways of representing thoughts, ideas and feelings which include music, painting, drawing, sculpture, dance, drama and role play. The younger the child the more likely that the preferred mode of representation will be physical (Matthews 1994). In order to support young children's learning effectively, teachers must encourage a range of representational forms across the curriculum and recognize that young children's play and exploration have a vital contribution to make to thought and creativity. Representing ideas in one form will support thinking in other media – reformulation of ideas supports development (Odam 1995; Mithen 1996).

It has been known for a long time that too early and too formal an introduction to standard systems of representation can hinder children's understanding of symbols (McMillan 1930; Board of Education 1933). More recently, Martin Hughes's work (1986) on children's understanding of mathematical symbols underlines the difficulties imposed on children when we fail to support their growing concept of the function of symbols. Kieran Egan's study (1988) of the development of thought in young children emphasizes the importance of exposing young children to a wide variety of representational forms. In short, children become more able to use abstract symbols effectively, including standard numbers and letters, if they have had opportunities to explore and communicate through a range of representational systems, including their own invented ones. They become more able to interpret the representations of others if they have first been encouraged to express their experience in their own chosen fashion.

Children have to learn that we can use a variety of media to represent ideas. Just as they learn to use language to express themselves because adults attribute meaning to their earliest babbling, so they must learn with the support of adults that pencil marks, musical sounds and three-dimensional shapes can represent ideas, feelings and thoughts.

In school a particular emphasis is placed on representing ideas as a record of learning. This is in part to enable teachers to assess children's progress, but it is sometimes unconsciously used as a mechanism for prolonging an activity or to keep children busily occupied. If children do not clearly understand the purposes for which they are recording their findings they may become disaffected, and the activity is therefore counter-productive.

Key words and phrases from the programmes of study (see p. 17)

In the early years, teachers must take care to ensure that the technical elements of representation are embedded in activities which have real purpose and that children are given the space for genuine communication of their own ideas. Standard forms of presentation will be more effectively taught and learned within such a context.

There are dangers in placing an emphasis on using cut-out shapes and other stereotyped images since these formulate other people's ideas and may inhibit children from developing genuine understanding of the communicative and expressive functions of representation and recording.

The term 'record' in the programmes of study is frequently used in conjunction with the form that the recording is to take, e.g. graphs, bar charts in science. As indicated above, children need a great deal of prior experience of recording in their own and a variety of other ways before formal outcomes can make any sense to them.

As many opportunities as possible should be found for promoting meaningful recording, and every area of the classroom should expose children to a wide variety of forms of representation. Mathematics provides many opportunities for children to record for a variety of purposes and in a range of ways (see Appendix 2, p. 41).

Examples of representing in practice

A farm visit may be represented through:

- dressing-up clothes and time for free play;
- bus, driver's cap, tickets and money;
- small world play;
- photographs and discussion of the visit (all forms of representation will be made more effective through discussion);
- children's drawings, paintings, models;
- other artists' representations of farms;
- soil and relevant implements in a tray;
- gardening activities outdoors;
- dance and movement;
- songs, stories, music and rhymes (known, adapted, improvised);
- class books and news.

English

Speaking and listening

1a • Tell stories, both real and imagined, imaginative play and drama

• Explore, develop and clarify ideas; predict outcomes and discuss possibilities

• Describe events, observations and experiences; make simple, clear explanations of choices, giving reasons for opinions and actions

2a Make themselves clear through organizing what they say

2b Use talk to develop thinking and extend ideas

3b Explore and discuss meanings of words

Reading

Writing

1a Write as a means of remembering, communicating, organizing and developing ideas and information

1b Write in response to a variety of stimuli (including personal experience)

2b Plan and review writing, assembling and developing their ideas on paper and on screen. Teachers should help them to compose at greater length by writing for them, demonstrating the way their ideas may be recorded in print

Mathematics

Using and applying mathematics

1b Explain their thinking to support the development of their reasoning

3b Relate numerals and other symbols to a range of situations

3c Discuss work

3d Use a variety of forms of mathematical presentation

Number

1a Record in a variety of ways, including ways that relate to mental work

Shape, space and measures

2a Describe and discuss shapes and patterns that can be seen and visualized

Science

General requirements

4a Use scientific vocabulary to name and describe living things, materials, phenomena and processes

4b Present scientific information through drawings, diagrams, tables, charts, speech and writing

Experimental and investigative science

1a Turn ideas (including their own) into a form that can be investigated

Physical processes

2a Describe the movement of familiar things

Design and technology

3c Develop ideas through shaping, assembling and rearranging materials

3d Develop and communicate ideas by making freehand drawings, and by modelling ideas in other ways

Geography

2 Observe, question, record, communicate ideas and inform

3b Undertake fieldwork activities e.g. mapping the school playground

3d Make maps and plans of real and imaginary places

REPRESENTING

Information technology

2a Generate and communicate pupils' ideas in different forms

3b Give direct signals or commands, and describe the effects of their actions

3c Use IT to explore aspects of real and imaginary situations

History

Key elements

5a Communicate awareness and understanding of history in a variety of ways

Physical education

Dance

3c Explore moods and feeling through dance

Music

4c Compose in response to a variety of stimuli

4d Communicate musical ideas to others

5g Use sounds to create musical effects

5h Record compositions using symbols, where appropriate

6d Respond to the changing character and mood of a piece of music by means of dance or other suitable forms of expression

6e Describe sounds in simple terms

Art

1 Experience different approaches to art

2a Express ideas and feelings

2b Record observations

2c Design and make images and artefacts

7a Record responses

The children are interested in Postman Pat: the teacher, having arranged a number of activities about letters and posting, is keen to bring in some IT activities. The Roamer is always popular with the children and so she decides to turn this piece of equipment into a 'Postman Pat' complete with black and white cat. As part of the developing activity children make houses with various construction materials, number them and then create their own road map. They write envelopes addressed to 'their' house. They are then given the task of programming the Postman Pat Roamer to follow an appropriate course to deliver the letters. Programming gets progressively more difficult when children realize that houses are numbered odd and even on different sides of the road, and they have to reprogram in order to make it as realistic as possible.

CHALLENGES FOR TEACHERS

PLAY

The place of play as intrinsic to a child's early learning has a clearly established position in the education of the under-fives. As recently as 1994, Ofsted fully expected these children to be involved in 'practical activity, enquiry and purposeful play'. No such requirement exists for children over 5 once they are subject to the National Curriculum. It is not surprising that teachers of children who are over 5 find themselves in the evident dilemma of being obliged to fulfil the requirements of the programmes of study while at the same time having to provide contexts for learning which are appropriate to the stage of development of their pupils. The result is that play is relegated in the classroom hierarchy, although it can motivate, interest and absorb children. Fisher (1996: 19) warns that it may be seen as 'ideal for using as a carrot in order to encourage children to finish the possibly less inspiring and motivating tasks set by the teacher'. Play is not an optional extra, nor is it the antithesis of 'work', even less a reward for completing some other less meaningful and absorbing task (Lindqvist 1995).

However, we should urge those who claim that play and the National Curriculum are 'uneasy bedfellows' (Abbott 1994) to think again. Indeed, part of the problem seems to lie in the nature of the word itself. There is no entirely satisfactory and agreed definition of play in an educational setting. This lack of agreement has sometimes led to educators suggesting that the word should be replaced in the school context. Their suggestions ('discovery activity' or 'exploring time' being just two of the many) suffer the same ambiguity as the word 'play', and are even less helpful. What we need is to talk about it, because although reaching a consensus definition of play is problematical,

> the discussion itself is a valuable and rewarding one
> . . . Indeed, if children are to experience consistency,
> coherence and quality in provision and in their
> interactions with adults, then discussion of what play
> is, and can be, is essential. It is equally valuable in a
> search for quality experiences to explore also what
> play is not: for example it is not simply everything a
> child does.
>
> (Abbott 1994: 78)

What play can provide indisputably is a vehicle for children's self-directed activity in which there is scope for their enterprise within a rich context for selecting, decision making and problem solving. Where appropriate, it can also allow a place for adult intervention and involvement. This is 'not a compromise nor a dilution of the notion of self-direction, but a recipe for the best learning processes and outcomes' (Dowling 1995: 74). Effective learning in early childhood is distinguished by being conceived of as a combination of four essential processes:

- *dynamic* – learning intrinsically bound up with activity – not just of the physical kind, but activity of the mind which engages with a situation and is immersed in it;
- *interactive* – learning which is an expansion of existing ways of conceiving the world in the light of alternative ways;
- *social* – children learn in partnership with other people. They adopt different learning stances – sometimes sharing the group consciousness, sometimes borrowing a role to find their place within the group situation; and
- *situational* – learning promoted by a stimulating context and through meaningful and purposeful activities.

All of these processes are to be found embodied in purposeful play activity. That purpose comes from a recognition of the potential for learning within any play situation, and ensuring that early childhood educators are clear about why they are providing a play context. In turn they can then be equally clear to parents, to sceptical colleagues and perhaps, most importantly, to the children themselves. Without this explanation, it is no wonder that children often make the response 'we just played' to parents' earnest request for a résumé of the child's day at school. There is a need to allocate time for reflection with children on their play activity and to discuss with them what it is they have learned.

In *First Class* (Ofsted 1993) inspectors reported that in reception classes visited, fewer than half of the teachers fully exploited the educational potential of play and that it often lacked an educational purpose: teachers over-directed work and under-directed play. Given that reception classes nationwide contain children whose ages range from just 4 to 5 years and three months, this is a vital stage for making a bridge through play-related activity between the curriculum provided for under-fives and that of the National Curriculum Key Stage 1. Yet some teachers seem to be overconcerned with formalizing learning and remain unconvinced of the power of play. As Rubin *et al.* (1983) have pointed out, play is unpredictable and irrational in the sense that it is not always realistic. Because it is pleasurable, and does not lead directly to pre-determined goals, play is often not seen to be serious or worthwhile.

These very risk factors are, however, almost always present when learning is at its most exciting in the classroom. The provision of a range of approaches to learning and the blending of children's self-directed activity with teacher-led instruction lead to success. Moyles's (1991: 15) 'play spiral' provides an excellent model showing how the process of learning is cyclical:

> rather like a pebble on a pond, the ripples from the exploratory free play through directed play and back to enhanced and enriched free play, allowed a spiral of learning spreading ever outwards into wider experiences for the children and upwards into the accretion of knowledge and skills. In defining play in

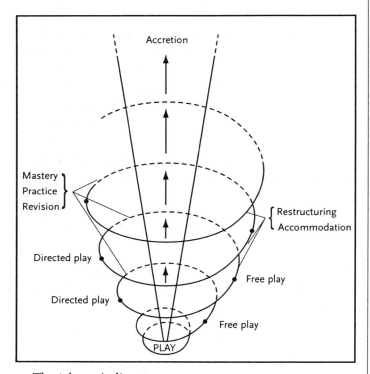

The 'play spiral'

this way, we are hopefully allowing ourselves to see its greater potential, freeing it from the constraints imposed by thinking too didactically about structure.

Teachers need to devote time to making the kind of careful observations of play activity which confirm its value in promoting children's learning.

Key words and phrases from the programmes of study

Close examination of the programmes of study for all the subjects in Key Stage 1 of the National Curriculum shows that the word 'play' is rarely mentioned. The English Orders do, however, state that pupils should be given opportunities to talk for a range of purposes, including 'using language appropriate to a role', and through 'imaginative play and drama'.

Similarly, although the specific teaching of elements of games play in PE is outside the scope of this discussion, it is easy to see how the practical processes required in many subjects could be gained through playful experience. The teacher's task is thus essentially one of *interpretation*, and there is no doubt that many aspects of all the subjects can be interpreted and presented to children through play activity. The essential proviso is that it should take children forward from where they are towards new understandings without fear of failure. Teachers can consider curriculum coverage 'not in terms of looking for a play curriculum but through viewing play as a process wherein children will exhibit certain behaviours' (Moyles 1991). Socio-dramatic play is particularly well suited to providing an exciting situation for learning, legitimized by the structure the teacher provides: 'it is often situated in contexts which by their very nature are event-structured rather than curriculum-structured. In other words, if you elect to create a travel agency then you take on board all the behaviours associated with travel agencies, not just those which narrowly reflect one area of the curriculum' (Hall and Abbott 1991: 4).

Play, then, provides a means to avoid children being constrained by prematurely formalized tasks, through an approach which allows them to perceive and take pleasure in their own progress. Much of the child's day is spent in responding to the direction of adults, but engaging in play allows children to regain the learning initiative. There is also a clear role for the adult educator. In allowing initiative to flourish, the teacher needs to have planned carefully, to have provided a stimulating context for learning and to be aware of the need for sensitive intervention. It is also important for early childhood educators to promote play through clear explanations of its potential and power for learning.

Fisher (1996: 30) describes her 'Charter for Play' thus:

A charter for play

1 Acknowledge its unique contribution as a process by which young children can learn.
2 Plan for it as an integral part of the curriculum and not an 'added extra'.
3 Facilitate it with appropriate high quality provision.
4 Act as a catalyst when intervention is appropriate and a scaffolder when expertise is needed.
5 Observe it in order to have first-hand evidence of children's learning.
6 Evaluate it in order to understand the needs of the learner better.
7 Value it through comment and commitment in order for its status in the classroom to be appreciated.
8 Fight for it with rigorous, professional argument in order to bring about deeper understanding and acceptance by colleagues, parents, governors and the community at large.

This set of statements provides an excellent basis for rigorous discussion within any school; it gives an opportunity to reconsider the place of play and to strengthen understanding about its role in implementing the National Curriculum.

If a charter can be influential in making educators re-examine where they stand on some key issues, then Nutbrown's (1996) reminder of the need for respectful educators who take account of the United Nations Charter on the Rights of the Child is very timely. In the same book (p. 98), David poses the question: 'If children's time and activities are constantly determined and organised by adults in their lives, how can they ever explore answers to their own questions about the world and about themselves? They are playing to live.'

As they interpret the National Curriculum, early childhood educators must ensure that this access to life and learning is considered, appropriately planned and provided for, and given status through play.

LEARNING OUTDOORS

Edgington (1998) has identified a number of reasons why it is essential to make full use of the school grounds, the immediate locality and the wider environment. Active learning outdoors is essential because:

- The most rapid physical development takes place during the first seven years, and children need opportunities to practise and refine their gross motor skills.
- Today's children have been found to be unfit. They need regular vigorous exercise for healthy heart development.
- Many children are denied safe outdoor play – often the nursery garden or school playground is the only place a child can play outside.
- Physical achievements make children feel good, and enhance their self-esteem.
- Some learning can only happen outdoors, such as learning about the weather, nature, what it feels like to be high or low on large apparatus, or how to use bikes and other wheeled toys. Learning across all areas of the curriculum can happen outside if it is planned and provided for.

In spite of a growing awareness of the importance of offering opportunities to be and learn outdoors, many young children's outdoor experience in school is limited to playtimes, with few if any resources, and in the company of older children – which may be intimidating. The earlier introduction of 4-year-olds into reception classes has focused attention on this issue, and many schools are developing their outdoor provision to offer all primary children access to purposeful play experiences at break times (Blatchford 1989) and other learning opportunities throughout the school day (Titman 1991).

Key words and phrases from the programmes of study

The programmes of study for science and geography demand that children experience learning outdoors. They require:

- a knowledge of plants and animals in the local environment;
- investigation of the physical and human features of the surroundings;

- fieldwork in the locality of the school.

Although there are no explicit requirements in other programmes of study, teachers should seek out as many opportunities as possible for exploiting the full potential of learning outside. They can be found within:

English – re-enactments through role play and visits;
music – exploring dynamics;
art – investigating pattern and texture in natural forms;
mathematics – understanding and using properties of position and movement; and purposeful contexts for measuring.

EQUAL OPPORTUNITIES ISSUES

Equality of opportunity is both a legal and a moral right. All children have an equal right to education, but this does not always mean the *same* opportunities. Because of their prior experiences, special needs or interests, children will require different support to gain access to the curriculum (Runnymede Trust 1993).

The National Curriculum claims to provide equality by defining children's entitlement under the law. There is a danger if all children are expected to learn the same content in the same way at the same pace; teachers must differentiate to take account of children's particular strengths and learning styles (see the section on the planning process which deals with differentiation, p. 24). There are some specific issues to be considered when planning for subjects of the National Curriculum. The following paragraphs cannot be exhaustive, but they are intended to alert teachers to these issues.

English

The emphasis placed on standard English has been viewed with some dismay by teachers of young children since it is vital to children's learning and self-esteem that we value their backgrounds, prior learning and the languages and dialects of homes and communities. There is a vast amount of research to suggest that supporting children's home language is the most effective way to promote learning, including the learning of standard forms of English (Engel and Whitehead 1996). Ways must be found to enable children to compare registers and accents, languages and dialects, so that in time they can choose from a repertoire. In fact the programmes of study require the inclusion of

stories and poems from a range of cultures and styles.

Although some research finds that boys do less well in English than girls, it is certain that their achievement is helped when teachers convince them of the value of what they are doing and create a wide range of opportunities for developing and using literacy (EOC/Ofsted 1996).

Mathematics

Girls have traditionally been thought to do less well in this area than boys, but are now being seen to outperform boys at every phase of education. They are helped by opportunities to apply mathematics purposefully and in meaningful contexts (EOC/Ofsted 1996).

Science

Children are required to recognize similarities and differences between themselves and others (life processes and living things 4a). This can be a useful starting point for a great deal of effective work on gender and culture.

Design and technology

Girls' experience in this area is sometimes less than that of boys in the early years. A study by the Equal Opportunities Commission and Ofsted (EOC/Ofsted 1996) suggests that girls' achievement can be boosted by focused teaching initiatives, but it also says that this does not so easily lead to an increase in confidence. It also indicates that girls have better ideas for technology – a strong case here for mixed groupings (Bennett and Dunne 1990). However, in order to contribute with confidence, it may be helpful for girls to work initially in single-sex groups (Browne and France 1986).

Information technology

Girls are less likely to have access to a computer than boys and, as with design and technology, teaching may have to focus on building confidence in girls.

History

There is an emphasis on British history. Women are explicitly mentioned in areas of study 2, and since many of the children in school have their roots in other countries, the area of study which talks about the changes in their own lives and those of their families will require consideration of history beyond these shores.

Geography

Opportunities to study places outside pupils' day-to-day experience are prescribed. Care should be taken to ensure that third-world stereotypes are not reinforced if an area outside Europe is chosen. Studying the locality enables children and their parents to value and possibly play a part in developing their environment. Such empowerment is an important aspect of equality of opportunity (Whalley 1995).

Physical education

Young children bring with them from the outside world some fixed views about what are appropriate activities for men and women. If left unchallenged, their introduction to institutionalized education may serve to reinforce their views. Their desire to belong to a club may cause them to behave in limiting ways. Thus boys who have happily bopped around at home may at school claim that dancing is only for girls, while girls may decline to get involved in the rough-and-tumble of ball play. Teachers of young children will need to be on the lookout for such stereotyping; they should challenge it actively through providing strong role models and images to act as a counterbalance.

Music

The Orders expressly require that music in a variety of styles, from different times and cultures and by well-known composers and performers, past and present, should be included alongside music from our diverse musical heritage. There is a vast range of music and songs available from all over the world, in a wide range of styles. There are folk songs which tell of the lives of ordinary working men and women in times gone by. The National Curriculum requires us to reflect this wonderful diversity.

Children and adults sometimes hold stereotyped views about which instruments are best suited to girls and boys. While being sensitive to subtle cultural differences, teachers should take care to challenge these views by making sure that girls get a chance to play the drums, and boys take their turn with the less impressive triangle or shaker. Pictures of adult musicians can be used to introduce new role models.

Art

Children should be introduced to the work of artists from a variety of cultures, and provision should introduce them to this breadth from the start. Many picture books are illustrated by women artists, who are often underrepresented as artists working in both two and three dimensions. Stimulus for artistic activities can be built on images and ideas from diverse sources. Teachers should however be aware of culturally determined attitudes to visual representation.

CROSS-CURRICULAR LINKS

Young children's learning is not compartmentalized into subjects (Bruce 1987; EYCG 1989), and many experiences provide opportunities for cross-curricular learning. We felt it was important to indicate some of the cross-curricular opportunities contained within the programmes of study. As Robin Alexander (1995) points out: 'conceptions of the problem of curricular scope and balance couched in terms of subject labels and time have severe limitations, and alternatives . . . emphasise the curriculum as experienced by pupils'.

The programmes of study in design and technology explicitly state that pupils should apply skills, knowledge and understanding from programmes of study for other subjects where appropriate. Our appendices specify potential cross-curricular links in other subjects of the National Curriculum too, which teachers should exploit in order to provide relevant and meaningful links with children's past experience and their way of constructing an understanding of the world.

The areas of learning used to define the DLOs are designed to feed into the early stages of the National Curriculum. Science, technology and the humanities are grouped together as aspects of children's growing knowledge and understanding of the world. Creative development incorporates music, drama, art and imaginative play. Physical development is included, and personal and social development permeates all aspects of children's learning. Mathematical learning as well as linguistic and literary development are seen to take place through a wide variety of activities. The DLOs provide a way of thinking about the curriculum in the early years which endorses cross-curricular work. They encompass opportunities for genuine cross-curricular learning, which continue to be important throughout Key Stage 1 and beyond.

Katz and Chard (1989) provide a strong rationale for cross-curricular work in the early years. They point out that this approach lends coherence and continuity to school work, and that knowledge and skills acquired through instruction are likely to be strengthened by being applied. Everyday life is not experienced in discrete categories, and young children's thinking is not defined by the constraints of subject boundaries. A rigidly subject-focused curriculum may cut across children's interests; learning is likely to be more effective when planned from a careful analysis of the cross-curricular potential of all the activities on offer within the classroom and outdoors.

An analysis of the examples used throughout this book shows that they all have a contribution to make in a variety of subject areas. Teachers can thus feel justified in planning in a cross-curricular way, and they can rely on their professional judgement to identify the proportion of time spent on specific subjects for their school's audit of percentages dedicated to the National Curriculum. Some teachers use their observations of pupils to identify learning that is taking place through self-chosen activities; they can provide a curricular analysis that is well founded in evidence. Rigorous records and systematic review allow them to ensure that each child is receiving his or her entitlement to the full National Curriculum without relying on a rigid planning framework. The 20 per cent of time that is available for individual schools to use as they wish can also make a legitimate contribution to flexibility, and allow for the possibility of revisiting a topic or area of learning where this will support children's growing understanding.

DEVELOPMENTALLY APPROPRIATE PLANNING

The early years curriculum has always embraced inclusive education in principle. The planning sheets which follow offer some examples of how National Curriculum programmes of study can be planned for and covered in ways which meet children's different developmental needs, including any identified special educational needs. One set of planning sheets starts from an area of provision (water) which should be available in all early years classes, and the other set starts from required content within a National Curriculum subject (mathematics). These sheets are not meant to be prescriptive. They are offered to highlight the complexity involved in planning the early years curriculum and to demonstrate the thinking processes required. In each case the process follows a similar pattern and moves through the three stages in planning i.e. long, medium and short term.

Long-term planning

is concerned with children's entitlement to a broad and balanced curriculum. It is achieved through the appropriate allocation of time to the teaching and assessment of the National Curriculum, religious education and other aspects of the curriculum identified by the school. Schools still need to decide when and how they will offer this prescribed content, and what additional content they feel will be necessary. The DLOs for children who have reached statutory school age provide guidance on the kind of knowledge, skills and attitudes children are expected to achieve before they start the National Curriculum. Staff working in reception and Year 1 classes will need to take account of these specified outcomes as well as the National Curriculum programmes of study, both in their planning and when making assessments of individual children.

Many primary schools are planning schemes of work which demonstrate how curriculum content will be covered during the Key Stage, but sometimes these schemes are too compartmentalized into discrete subjects, too dependent on published schemes and worksheets, and they take too little account of the needs of the children in a particular class. At every stage of the planning process, teachers need to be guided by what they know about child development and what they know interests and motivates children. Planning should always be flexible enough to enable individual teachers to match their teaching to the specific needs and interests of the children in their group; these details are addressed at the short-term planning stage.

The long-term planning sheet showing the potential of water play (Table 1, p. 28) shows how Key Stage 1 staff could consider how curriculum content could be covered within activities which have traditionally been provided in infant classes. In this example, we have taken water play and highlighted which concepts and skills could be covered if full use is made of this area of provision. We have included important curriculum content which is not in the National Curriculum, and indicated cross-curricular links in other subjects such as PE and IT. This type of long-term planning helps teachers to realize the full potential of motivating play provision, and to exploit this potential in their medium and short-term planning of both adult- and child-initiated experiences (see Table 2, p. 29).

Planning can also start from a National Curriculum subject. In this case staff teams need to plan how the various elements of each subject will be mapped over the terms of children's nursery and infant experience, to ensure breadth and balance in the curriculum.

Medium-term planning

addresses continuity and progression from one stage in each subject to the next, and from one class or school to the next. Medium-term plans set out what is to be covered during a term or half-term. Teachers identify intended learning (the concepts, skills, knowledge and attitudes) for this period from the school's schemes of work or directly from the National Curriculum programmes of study. Decisions about suitable content need to be influenced by each teacher's knowledge of the previous term's work, and the assessments which have been made of the children in the class. There is little point in forging ahead when children have not yet grasped content introduced previously.

In the medium-term planning sheets, we have demonstrated how the long-term plans for water play and for mathematics might be developed. The medium-term plan for water (Table 3, p. 30) takes science as the focus for learning but also identifies cross-curricular learning possibilities. The plan for mathematics (Table 4, p. 31) shows how, when children are engaged in the range of planned activities which could be offered for mathematical learning, they may also access other curriculum content. In both examples extension possibilities are identified to show how teachers might develop activities to encompass additional learning.

This approach to medium-term planning should enable teachers to be more aware of the range of learning which can develop from one starting point. It can also highlight a broader range of assessment opportunities, and help them to manage time more effectively.

Short-term planning

focuses on what will be taught this week or on a particular day, and draws on the medium-term plan made for the term or half-term. It must take account of children's prior learning and experience and must be *differentiated* to take account of the varying developmental levels within any group of children. This idea suggests that the younger the children and the shorter their time in school, the less homogeneous a group they will be. When planning both learning intentions and the activities which will best enable children to achieve the desired outcome, it is necessary for teachers to take account of the following factors:

- children's previous life experience both in- and outside school – this is essential if experiences offered are to be relevant;
- developmental and learning needs – this should include any special educational needs;
- language needs of bilingual children – they should receive support in their home language as well as English;
- approaches to learning – these include self-esteem, motivation, interests and degree of enthusiasm, confidence and ability to work with others.

The short-term planning sheets in Tables 5 and 6 both demonstrate how teachers can differentiate their planning of specific curriculum content for three groups of children. Both sheets follow the same format to demonstrate the thinking processes necessary (n.b. although teachers need to go through the same detailed thought processes, they may not need to write in the same degree of detail).

Previous experience/prior learning – this section highlights what children need to know and understand, and what skills they need to have, if they are to be able to access the intended learning planned by the teacher. It also includes relevant life experience which would make an activity particularly motivating to the children concerned.

Intended learning – this section highlights specific learning intentions for each group of children.

Activity – this section describes the activities which have been planned to give children access to the intended learning. Teachers need to consider how their planned activities are likely to motivate the children concerned; if one activity does not interest a child it is always possible to offer an alternative to help the child achieve the intended learning. In the water example (Table 5, p. 32), the children will all be doing a similar activity but the degree of complexity, and demands made, vary according to children's life experience and ability. In the plan for mathematical learning (Table 6, p. 33) the children will be engaged in different activities designed to help them work towards the intended outcome. This section should also show whether and where children will be supported by an adult, and specify the focus of the teacher's activity.

Resources – this section lists the resources required for the specific activity and acts as an *aide memoire* for staff.

Evidence and *Assessment* – these sections highlight the methods by which teachers will gain evidence that children are achieving the intended learning and the possibilities for assessing children's learning within other subject areas.

ASSESSMENT

The assessment of children is an integral part of the education process. Teachers need to know what children understand and can do in order to plan effectively for development and progress. Good assessment is based on:

- observation of children in action;
- discussion with children while they are reflecting on their actions during and/or after an activity;
- outcomes of children's activity; e.g. writing, models, photographs.

All of these provide *evidence* of learning.

The younger the child, the less tangible the evidence of learning and the more the teacher has to rely on observation and discussion. Photographs and work samples, adequately annotated, provide other ways of capturing the evidence on which judgements are based. Children's writing is not always a reliable and informative indicator of their understanding because there is a wide gulf between what young children understand and what they can write. Worksheets probably offer the least accurate evidence of all, as they are often an obstacle course for children attempting to represent their learning in ways which make sense to them rather than in those prescribed by the adult.

Although some frameworks for baseline assessment will need careful interpretation to avoid distorting work with children as they start compulsory school, the requirements for ongoing teacher assessment during Key Stage 1 are mostly compatible with effective early years practice. In order to assess children using the level descriptions for levels 1–3 it is necessary for teachers to:

- create a well-organized and well-resourced learning environment where independence, first-hand experience and play are valued and fostered, where children are encouraged to think for themselves, generate ideas, make choices and experiment, and where talk is encouraged. N.b. for science and geography it is essential that children work and are assessed outdoors as well as in the classroom;
- include observation opportunities in their weekly and daily planning;
- assess within the full range of activities, both child- and adult-initiated (e.g. for maths AT1 children should be taught and assessed 'as an integral part of classroom activities'), and within a range of social contexts both with and without an adult;
- observe in a range of contexts – with and without an adult;
- listen to and note down children's comments, descriptions, explanations, questions, responses to questions, ideas, reflections, retelling of stories, etc.;
- notice children's strategies for problem solving;
- analyse children's attainments, such as pieces of independent writing, models, and the use of mathematical understanding, especially when achieved in play as well as during teacher-directed sessions.

All of these assessment processes inform the teacher about what children know and can do. However, they are only of value if this information is then used to refine future planning. In the light of the assessments they have made, teachers regularly need to make decisions about whether their planning is still relevant and appropriate.

THE WAY FORWARD

This book has reminded us, as practitioners privileged to engage with young children, that we must respect their abilities. We owe it to them to sustain their natural curiosity and enthusiasm for learning. We cannot allow the National Curriculum to become an excuse for working inappropriately and thus ineffectively in the early years. The ways of working outlined in this book are entirely compatible with the statutory requirements and can lead to higher levels of attainment. Analysis of research (Ball 1995) suggests that a very early concentration on formal approaches to the curriculum can constrain and impede children's learning. The authors trust that teachers and other adults with an interest in the early years will find this book supportive as they make responsible decisions about their own practice and explain their professional work to others who are less knowledgeable about the early years curriculum.

This will involve sharing insights and information about the nature of play, its significant role in children's social and intellectual development, and the essentially interactive characteristics of all worthwhile learning. Only a rich interpretation of the National Curriculum at Key Stage 1 can provide the foundation for lifelong learning, personal development, and those skills and abilities on which the future of our society depends.

TABLES 1–6: PLANNING GUIDES

Table 1 Long-term planning (topic): water

ENGLISH

Concepts

- communication

Skills

Speaking and listening

- explaining, developing, clarifying ideas
- predicting outcomes and discussing possibilities
- describing events, observations and experiences
- making simple, clear explanations of choices
- giving reasons for opinions and actions
- asking and answering questions that clarify understanding
- using task to develop thinking and extending ideas in light of discussion
- developing vocabulary through activities that encourage interest in words

MATHEMATICS

Concepts

- capacity
- measures: weight, volume
- shape
- time

Skills

- measuring
- classifying
- sorting
- counting
- collecting, recording and interpreting data

SCIENCE

Concepts

- properties of water
- floating and sinking
- properties/changes of materials
- forces

Skills

- observing
- questioning
- predicting
- hypothesizing
- reasoning
- testing
- explaining

DESIGN AND TECHNOLOGY

Concepts

- health and safety

Skills

- disassembling different products
- generating ideas
- using simple mechanisms

INFORMATION TECHNOLOGY

Skills

- using IT to record outcomes

HISTORY

Concepts

- change over time

Skills

- using appropriate historical language
- sequencing

GEOGRAPHY

Concepts

- location
- water transport

Skills

- using geographical terms
- following directions

MUSIC

Concepts

- quality of sound
- understanding that sound can be made in different ways

Skills

- exploring and creating sound

ART

Concepts

- shape, form and space
- pattern and texture

Skills

- expressing ideas and feelings

Table 2 Long-term planning (subject): mathematics

TERM 1	TERM 2
sorting	space/shape: triangle, square, circle, rectangle
grouping	pattern
positional vocabulary	measures: light/heavy, long/short
sequencing	capacity: full/empty

TERM 3	TERM 4
comparison using appropriate language	measures: length – less/more than 1 m
non-standard units	capacity – half full/empty
shapes: 2-D, 3-D	time – o'clock/half past
simple coordinates	geometric features of shapes
data handling	copy, continue and make patterns

TERM 5	TERM 6
standard measures: time/weight/capacity/money	data collection
angle: the concept of 'half'; 1/2 turns; right angles	handling/recording/interpreting data
symmetry	number patterns and coordinates
rotation	reading and interpreting numbers and scales

Ongoing number; =, x, −, ÷; mental mathematics
All units of work taught through 'using and applying mathematics'

Table 3 Medium-term planning (topic): water

Intended learning	Activity	Resources	Cross-curricular links	Extension
SCIENCE *Experimental and investigative science* • plan experimental work (1) • obtain evidence (2) • consider evidence (3) *Materials and their properties* • sort materials into groups on the basis of simple properties (1b) • recognize and name common types of materials (1c) • choose materials for specific uses on the basis of their properties (1e) *Physical processes* • understand that forces can make things speed up or slow down or change direction (2c)	• make boats that can float and move on water	• water tray (inside or out), paddling pool, water • materials, e.g. plasticine, plastic, foil, wood, fabric, balloons, lolly sticks, straws, tissue paper, glue, felts, sellotape, string, rubber bands	**ENGLISH** *Writing* • record outcomes using IT (2b) **MATHEMATICS** *Using and applying mathematics* • trial distance boats travel/loads carried (2b) • find out whether all boats made of plastic float? • use mathematical language (3a) *Shape, space and measures* • recognize movement (3a) • compare e.g. objects (4a) **DESIGN AND TECHNOLOGY** whole of D&T PoS **ART** e.g. • experience different approaches to art, craft and design (1) • express ideas (2a) • record observations (2b) • design and make images and artefacts (2c) • learn about the use of shape, form and space (4d) • safely use materials, tools and techniques for practical work (6) • gather and use resources and materials to generate ideas (7b) • explore and use 2-D and 3-D media (7c) • review and modify work (7d) • respond to and evaluate own and others' work (7f) • recognize images as sources of ideas (8b) • use source material as a basis for work (8c) • experiment with tools and techniques (8d) • review work and describe what could be changed or developed (8f)	**ENGLISH** *Reading* • reference materials (1b) • stories (e.g. *Mr Gumpy's Outing*) (1a) *Writing* • plan and/or record process (2b) • plan and/or record results **GEOGRAPHY** • use geographical terms (3a) • undertake fieldwork e.g. visit river, canal, pond, sea, harbour (link to study of locality) and/or thematic study (3b) • follow directions (3c) **MUSIC** e.g. • music relevant to voyages, travelling by boat: • from different times and cultures (3a) • by well-known composers (3b) • recognize musical elements of timbre (2e) • explore, create and select sounds (5f) • recognize how sounds can be made in different ways (6a) • describe the sounds they have made or listened to (6e)

Table 4 Medium-term planning (subject): mathematics

Intended learning	Activity	Cross-curricular links	Extension
Using and applying mathematics • practical tasks (1a) • explain thinking (1b) • use appropriate mathematical equipment (2b) • record simple patterns and readiness to make predictions (4a) *Number* know addition and subtraction facts to 20, and develop a range of mental methods for finding, from known facts, those that they cannot recall (3c)	*Using and applying mathematics* • design a life-sized board game involving counting forward and backwards (1a/b) • design a small apparatus activity involving aiming and counting (child-identified scores) (2b) *Number* • develop a class shop where children role play shopkeeper and customer (1a) and give receipts (4a) • game in pairs; outside; throw two giant-sized dice to record outcomes (4a) • real problem-solving exercise, e.g. plan class picnic using school-grown produce. Each group to collect data on numbers attending picnic, numbers who like/dislike radishes, numbers who need alternative provision (5b) *Shape, space and measures* • cook, choose recipe to reinforce intended learning outcomes (4a/b)	**ENGLISH** *Writing* • organize and present writing in different ways (1c) • plan and review writing (2b) **SCIENCE** • general requirements **DESIGN AND TECHNOLOGY** • draw on own experience to generate ideas (3a) • clarify ideas through discussion (3b) • develop ideas through shaping, assembling and rearranging materials and components (3c) • develop and communicate design ideas (3d) • make suggestions (3e) **HISTORY** *Key elements* • use photographs of museum, shops (3/4) **GEOGRAPHY** • undertake fieldwork activities in the locality of the school (3b) • follow directions (3c) • make maps and plans of real and imaginary places using pictures and symbols (3d) **PHYSICAL EDUCATION** *General requirements* • be physically active (1a) • observe conventions of fair play (2a) *Games* • play simple competitive games (1a) • develop and practise a variety of ways of sending, receiving and travelling with a ball (1b) • perform in different ways basic actions of travelling, etc. (2a) **ART** • experience different approaches to art, craft and design (1) • record observations (2b) • design and make images and artefacts (2c)	**SCIENCE** *Physical processes* • describe the movement of familiar things (2a) • know that pushes and pulls are examples of forces (2b) **GEOGRAPHY** • use geographical terms (3a) • learn how quality of environment can be sustained and improved (6c) **DESIGN AND TECHNOLOGY** • designing and making skills (3/4f) **ART** • communicate visual ideas (3)

Table 5 Short-term planning (topic): water (showing differentiation)

Previous experience/ prior learning	The class is organized into three distinct groups based on the children's previous experience of: • exploring properties of materials • sorting materials into groups on the basis of simple properties • play with boats and water • stories, songs and rhymes with relevant vocabulary		
	A	**B**	**C**
Intended learning	• explore and select materials and equipment • use skills such as cutting, joining and building for a variety of purposes (DLO)	Experimental and investigative science • plan experimental work • obtain evidence • consider evidence	• predict and test the appropriateness of selected materials • record findings on computer
Activity	• observation using available materials and tools in self-selected ways	• make and test a model boat	• devise and carry out a fair test to determine the most appropriate paper for boat building
Resources	scissors, sellotape, glue, staples, walnut shells, plastic bowls, seashells, books/visual aids, artefacts		aquarium tank of water, limited range of paper, scissors, glue, staples, string, sellotape
Evidence	can be drawn from: • observing appropriateness of the materials and equipment selected • observing skills, e.g. exploring, selecting, collaborating, hypothesizing, sticking, cutting, testing, evaluating • discussing, in order to reveal child's strategies for making decisions re. materials and process • discussing, in order to assess child's use of language • discussing the outcome to establish child's perspective on what has been experienced/achieved • recording: a photograph of outcomes, if appropriate (adequately annotated) • recording: an evaluation of the outcome in the light of previous achievement and to identify progress/development in conceptual understanding (about materials) • recording: skill acquisition/consolidation/ development • recording: use of language	• observing how effectively child plans, obtains evidence and evaluates evidence • observing skills, e.g. exploring, selecting, collaborating, hypothesizing, sticking, cutting, testing, evaluating • discussing, in order to assess child's strategies for planning, obtaining evidence, considering evidence • discussing, in order to assess child's use of appropriate (subject-specific) language • discussing the outcome in order to assess the child's ability to evaluate in the light of their own evidence • recording: a photograph of outcome, if appropriate (adequately annotated) • recording: an evaluation of the outcome in the light of previous achievement, to identify progress in conceptual understanding	• observing appropriateness of the materials and equipment selected • observing appropriateness of the testing procedure • observing skills of predicting, hypothesizing, testing, evaluating • observing appropriateness of the use of a computer to record findings • discussing choice of materials • discussing strategies for making decisions about fair testing • discussing appropriateness of the selected format for recording process and outcome • recording: a photograph of outcome, if appropriate (adequately annotated) • recording: an evaluation of the processes selected in the light of previous attempts at fair testing • recording: an evaluation of the outcome in terms of the appropriateness of selected materials • recording: an evaluation of the selected format for recording
Assessment	involves evaluating the extent to which children have achieved the intended learning. Teachers should be aware that some children will have achieved beyond the teacher's intentions, and there will be achievement in other areas, e.g. maths, English, IT, D&T, art, etc.		

Table 6 Short-term planning (subject): mathematics (showing differentiation)

Previous experience/ prior learning	• familiarity with mathematical language • ability to count to 20 (at least) • one-to-one correspondence • sequencing	• grouping • familiarity with number rhymes, songs, stories • working with others • play experience without set task • role play	• the rules of games playing • taking turns • cooperation (PSE) • experience of recording in a variety of ways • life experiences
Intended learning	**A** through practical activities . . . develop awareness of number operations such as addition and subtraction (DLO)	**B** Number 1a, c, 5b begin to learn addition and subtraction facts to 20	**C** Number 1a, d, 5b develop a range of mental methods for finding from known facts those that they cannot recall
Activity	1 children design small apparatus games involving aiming 2 record in own way scores of 'hit' or 'miss' 3 follow by discussion with adult focused on addition and subtraction	• children work in pairs with two or three giant dice • teacher determines operations according to children's ability (e.g. add two dice and subtract one) • children throw dice to obtain two or three numbers for addition and/or subtraction • children record operations in own way • children use highlighters to identify particular bonds (e.g. odd/even numbers; all bonds to 16)	• set up class shop where items are priced in multiples of £1 (up to £20) • children to role play shopkeeper and customer • teacher to model appropriate behaviour • teacher to set a range of tasks controlling the amount of money given to the customer and/or number of purchases • shopkeeper provides receipt which records transactions for later discussion
Resources	• outdoor space • small apparatus, e.g. hoops, bean bags, skittles, sponge balls, buckets • recording materials, e.g. clipboard, paper, pencils, white board, pens	• outdoor space • two or three giant dice (with different numbering) • recording materials, e.g. clipboard, paper, pencils, white board, pens	• space (the equivalent of one table and six chairs!) • items for sale • money • swipe machines • cheque books • credit cards • till • bags for produce • purses • receipt book (duplicate)
Evidence	can be drawn from: • observing the way in which each child chooses to record • observing whether each child counts on or starts again at 1 • discussing why the child selected certain strategies • questioning how child arrived at the 'score'; what would happen if they had missed twice, etc. • recording: does the child's recording show that they recognize numbers, can write numbers and can add and/or subtract numbers accurately?	• observing each child's ability to apply number bonds to their game • observing each child's ability to categorize bonds which arise during the game • observing the child's confidence in challenging inaccurate or inappropriate answers • discussing why the child selected certain strategies • questioning how the child arrived at the 'score' • questioning to find out what the child understands about e.g. odd/even numbers, number bonds to 16 • recording: does the child show that they can add and subtract accurately? • recording: does highlighting show that the child understands number patterns, odd and even numbers and number bonds?	• observing each child's ability to draw on known number bonds to add prices and give change • observing the range of strategies used by each child to solve problems in the play situation • discussing number operations while in a role play situation • recording: do the shopkeeper's receipts record transactions accurately? • recording: do the receipts reflect the child's ability to make use of known number bonds in order to calculate unknown number bonds? • recording: do receipts show a range of ways of calculating transactions?
Assessment	involves evaluating the extent to which children have achieved the intended learning. Teachers should be aware that some children will have achieved beyond the teacher's intentions, and there will be achievement in other areas, e.g. maths, English, IT, D&T, art, etc.		

APPENDICES: ANALYSIS OF NATIONAL CURRICULUM PROGRAMMES OF STUDY

For an explanation of the symbols, please see page 3.

1 ENGLISH

Pupils' abilities should be developed within an integrated programme of speaking and listening, reading and writing. Pupils should be given opportunities that interrelate the requirements of the range, key skills, and standard English and language study sections.

Speaking and listening

	Active	Interactive	Decision making	Reflecting	Representing	Play	Outdoor	Equal opportunities	Cross-curricular links
■ 1 Range									
a Pupils should be given opportunities to talk for a range of purposes, including:									
■ telling stories, both real and imagined; imaginative play and drama; reading and listening to nursery rhymes and poetry, learning some by heart; reading aloud;	✓	00				✓		✓	History, geography
■ exploring, developing and clarifying ideas; predicting outcomes and discussing possibilities;	✓	✓		✓	✓				History, geography, design and technology
■ describing events, observations and experiences; making simple, clear explanations of choices; giving reasons for opinions and actions.	✓	✓	✓	✓	✓	00	00		History, geography, science, design and technology
b Pupils should be given opportunities to consider how talk is influenced by the purpose and by the intended audience. These opportunities should include work in groups of different sizes, and talking and presenting work to different audiences, including friends, the class, the teacher and other adults in the school.	✓	✓						✓	
c Pupils should be taught to listen carefully and to show their understanding of what they see and hear by making relevant comments. In considering what has been heard, pupils should be encouraged to remember specific points that interested them, and to listen to others' reactions.	✓				00				00
d Pupils should be encouraged to participate in drama activities, improvisation and performances of varying kinds, using language appropriate to a role or situation. They should be given opportunities to respond to drama they have watched, as well as that in which they have participated.	✓	00						✓	
■ 2 Key skills									
a To communicate effectively, pupils should be taught the importance of language that is clear, fluent and interesting. Building on their previous experience, pupils should be encouraged to speak with confidence, making themselves clear through organizing what they say and choosing words with precision. They should be taught to incorporate relevant detail in explanations, descriptions and narratives, and to distinguish between the essential and the less important, taking into account the needs of their listeners. Pupils should be taught conventions of discussion and conversation, e.g. taking turns in speaking, and how to structure their talk in ways that are coherent and understandable.	✓	✓		✓	✓	00	00	✓	Science, design and technology, art, music, history, geography

		Active	Interactive	Decision making	Reflecting	Representing	Play	Outdoor	Equal opportunities	Cross-curricular links
b	Pupils should be encouraged to listen with growing attention and concentration, to respond appropriately and effectively to what they have heard, and to ask and answer questions that clarify their understanding and indicate thoughtfulness about the matter under discussion. They should use talk to develop their thinking and extend their ideas in the light of discussion. They should be encouraged to relate their contributions in a discussion to what has gone before, taking different views into account.	✓	✓	✓	✓	✓				Science, design and technology, art, music, history, geography
■ 3	**Standard English and language study**									
a	Pupils should be introduced with appropriate sensitivity to the importance of standard English. Pupils should be given opportunities to consider their own speech and how they communicate with others, particularly in more formal situations or with unfamiliar adults. Pupils should be encouraged to develop confidence in their ability to adapt what they say to their listeners and to the circumstances, beginning to recognize how language differs, e.g. the vocabulary of standard English and that of dialects, how their choice of language varies in different situations. They should be introduced to some of the features that distinguish standard English, including subject–verb agreement and the use of the verb 'to be' in past and present tenses. Pupils may speak in different accents, but they should be taught to speak with clear diction and appropriate intonation.		!			00			✓	
b	Pupils' vocabulary should be extended through activities that encourage their interest in words, including exploration and discussion of:									
	■ the meanings of words and their use and interpretation in different contexts;	✓	00							
	■ words with similar and opposite meanings	✓	00							
	■ word games	✓	00				00			
	■ words associated with specific occasions, e.g. greetings, celebrations	✓	00		✓					
	■ characteristic language in story telling, e.g. 'Once upon a time'	✓	00		✓		00			

Reading programmes of study

■ 1 Range

		Active	Interactive	Decision making	Reflecting	Representing	Play	Outdoor	Equal opportunities	Cross-curricular links
a	Pupils should be given extensive experience of children's literature. They should read on their own, with others and to the teacher, from a range of genres that includes stories, poetry, plays and picture books. Pupils should read their own writing to the teacher and to others.	✓	✓		✓		00		✓	All
b	Pupils should be introduced to and should read information, both in print and on screen. They should be encouraged to make use of a range of sources of information, including dictionaries, IT-based reference materials, encyclopaedias and information presented in fictional form.	✓	✓	00	00				00	All
c	The materials read and discussed should be used to stimulate pupils' imagination and enthusiasm. They should include some or all of these features:	✓	✓						✓	All
	■ interesting subject matter and settings, which may be related to pupils' own experience or extend beyond their knowledge of the everyday;						00		✓	All

	Active	Interactive	Decision making	Reflecting	Representing	Play	Outdoor	Equal opportunities	Cross-curricular links
▪ a clear viewpoint, with accessible themes and ideas;				00					
▪ clarity of expression and use of language that benefits from being read aloud and reread;		00		00					
▪ language with recognizable repetitive patterns, rhyme and rhythm;				00					
▪ straightforward characterization and plot;				00				✓	
▪ the use of a variety of organizational and presentational techniques;				00					
▪ illustrations that are visually stimulating and enhance the words of the text.				00				✓	
d The literature read should cover the following categories:									
▪ poems and stories with familiar settings and those based on imaginary or fantasy worlds;		?			00	00		✓	History, geography
▪ books and poems written by significant children's authors;		?			00	00		✓	History, geography
▪ retellings of traditional folk and fairy stories;		?			00	00		✓	History, geography
▪ stories and poems from a range of cultures;		?			00	00		✓	History, geography
▪ stories, poems and chants containing patterned and predictable language;		?			00	00		✓	History, geography
▪ stories and poems that are particularly challenging in terms of length or vocabulary.		?			00	00		✓	History, geography
■ 2 Key skills									
a Pupils should be taught to read with fluency, accuracy, understanding and enjoyment, building on what they already know. In order to help them develop understanding of the nature and purpose of reading, they should be given an extensive introduction to books, stories and words in print around them. Pupils should be taught the alphabet, and be made aware of the sounds of spoken language in order to develop phonological awareness. They should also be taught to use various approaches to word identification and recognition, and to use their understanding of grammatical structure and the meaning of the text as a whole to make sense of print.	✓	00	00	✓	00			✓	All
b Within a balanced and coherent programme, pupils should be taught to use the following knowledge, understanding and skills: *Phonic knowledge*, focusing on the relationships between print symbols and sound patterns. Opportunities should be given for:									
▪ recognizing alliteration, sound patterns and rhyme, and relating these to patterns in letters;	00	00			00	00			
▪ considering syllables in longer words;				?					
▪ identifying initial and final sounds in words;				?	00				
▪ identifying and using a comprehensive range of letters and sounds, including combinations of letters, blends and digraphs, and paying specific attention to their use in the formation of words;	00	00		00	00				

	Active	Interactive	Decision making	Reflecting	Representing	Play	Outdoor	Equal opportunities	Cross-curricular links
▪ recognizing inconsistencies in phonic patterns;				00		✓			
▪ recognizing that some letters do not always produce a sound themselves but influence the sound of others.				?					
Graphic knowledge, focusing on what can be learned about word meanings and parts of words from consistent letter patterns, including:				?	?				
▪ plurals;		?		?	?				
▪ spelling patterns in verb endings;		?		?	?				
▪ relationships between root words and derivatives, e.g. help, helpful;		?		?	?				
▪ prefixes and suffixes.		?		?	?				
Word recognition, focusing on the development of a vocabulary of words recognized and understood automatically and quickly. This should extend from a few words of personal importance to a larger number of words from books and the environment. Pupils should be shown how to use their sight vocabulary to help them read words that have similar features. They should discuss alternative meanings of words and phrases.		00		00				?	
Grammatical knowledge, focusing on the way language is ordered and organized into sentences (syntax). Pupils should be shown how to use their knowledge of word order and the structure of written language to confirm or check meaning. Pupils should be taught to recognize the value of surrounding text in identifying unknown words. They should be taught to:	00				00				All
▪ check the accuracy of their reading, attending to whether it sounds right and/or makes sense grammatically;	✓	00	00	✓					All
▪ reread and/or read ahead passages when the sense has been lost.	✓	00	00	✓					All
Contextual understanding, focusing on meaning derived from the text as a whole. In order to confirm the sense of what they read, pupils should be taught to use their knowledge of book conventions, story structure, patterns of language and presentational devices, and their background knowledge and understanding of the content of a book. They should be taught to keep the overall sense of a passage in mind as a checking device.					00				All
c In understanding and responding to stories and poems, pupils should be given opportunities to:									
▪ talk about characters, events and language in books, beginning to use appropriate terminology;	00	✓		00	00				All
▪ say what might happen next in a story;	00	00		00					All
▪ retell stories;	00	00				00			All
▪ explain the content of a passage or whole text;	00	✓		00					All
▪ choose books to read individually and with others;	00	✓		00					All
▪ review their reading with their teacher;	00	✓		00					All
▪ read complete short texts, including playscripts;	00	00							All
▪ reread favourite stories and poems, learning some by heart;	✓								All

	Active	Interactive	Decision making	Reflecting	Representing	Play	Outdoor	Equal opportunities	Cross-curricular links
■ hear stories and poems read aloud frequently and regularly, including some longer, more challenging material;	00	00							All
■ prepare, present and act out stories and poems they have read.	00	00	00	00	00	00			All
d Pupils should be taught to use reference materials for different purposes. They should be taught about the structural devices for organizing information, e.g. contents, headings, captions.	✓	00	✓	00	00				All
■ 3 Standard English and language study Pupils should be given opportunities to consider the characteristics and features of different kinds of texts, e.g. beginnings and endings in stories. They should be taught to use their knowledge about language gained from reading, to develop their understanding of standard English.	✓	?		✓				?	

Writing

■ 1 Range

	Active	Interactive	Decision making	Reflecting	Representing	Play	Outdoor	Equal opportunities	Cross-curricular links
a Pupils should be helped to understand the value of writing as a means of remembering, communicating, organizing and developing ideas and information, and as a source of enjoyment. Pupils should be taught to write independently on subjects that are of interest and importance to them.	✓	00		00	✓	00		✓	All
b Pupils should be given opportunities to write in response to a variety of stimuli, including stories, poems, classroom activities and personal experience. Pupils should be taught to identify the purpose for which they write and to write for a range of readers, e.g. their teacher, their family, their peers, themselves.	✓	✓	✓	✓	✓	00	00	✓	All
c Pupils should be taught to organize and present their writing in different ways, helpful to the purpose, task and reader. They should be taught to write in a range of forms, incorporating some of the different characteristics of those forms. The range should include a variety of narratives, e.g. stories, diaries; poems; notes, e.g. lists, captions; records, e.g. observations; and messages, e.g. notices, invitations, instructions.	✓	✓	00	00	✓	00	00	✓	All

■ 2 Key skills

	Active	Interactive	Decision making	Reflecting	Representing	Play	Outdoor	Equal opportunities	Cross-curricular links
a Pupils should be taught to write with confidence, fluency and accuracy. They should be taught to differentiate between print and pictures, to understand the connections between speech and writing, and to learn about the different purposes and functions of written language. Pupils should be introduced to the alphabetic nature of writing and be taught to discriminate between letters, learning to write their own name. Pupils' early experiments and independent attempts at communicating in writing, using letters and known words, should be encouraged.	✓	00	00	00	✓	00		✓	All
b Pupils should have opportunities to plan and review their writing, assembling and developing their ideas on paper and on screen. Teachers should, on occasions, help pupils to compose at greater length by writing for them, demonstrating the ways that ideas may be recorded in print. To encourage confidence and independence, pupils should be given opportunities to collaborate, to read their work aloud and to discuss the quality of what is written. Pupils should be helped to make choices about vocabulary and to organize imaginative and factual writing in different ways, e.g. a cumulative pattern in a poem, a list of ingredients for a cake.	✓	✓	✓	✓	✓			✓	All

		Active	Interactive	Decision making	Reflecting	Representing	Play	Outdoor	Equal opportunities	Cross-curricular links
c	In punctuation, pupils should be taught that punctuation is essential to help a reader understand what is written. Pupils should be given opportunities to read their work aloud in order to understand the connections between the punctuation of a sentence and intonation and emphasis. Pupils should be taught to punctuate their writing, be consistent in their use of capital letters, full stops and question marks, and begin to use commas.	✓	00		✓					All
d	In spelling, pupils should be taught to:									
	■ write each letter of the alphabet;	✓				00	00			
	■ use their knowledge of sound-symbol relationships and phonological patterns;	✓				00				All
	■ recognize and use simple spelling patterns;	✓			00	00				All
	■ write common letter strings within familiar and common words;				?	?	00			All
	■ spell commonly occurring simple words;	?			00					
	■ spell words with common prefixes and suffixes.	?			00					
	Pupils should be taught to check the accuracy of their spelling, and to use word books and dictionaries, identifying initial letters as the means of locating words. They should be given opportunities to experiment with the spelling of complex words and to discuss misapplied generalisations and other reasons for misspellings. Close attention should be paid to word families.	00	00	00	00	00				All
e	In handwriting, pupils should be taught to hold a pencil comfortably in order to develop a legible style that follows the conventions of written English, including:	?								All
	■ writing from left to right and from top to bottom of the page;	?								All
	■ starting and finishing letters correctly;	?								All
	■ regularity of size and shape of letters;	?								All
	■ regularity of spacing of letters and words.	?								All
	They should be taught the conventional ways of forming letters, both lower case and capitals. They should build on their knowledge of letter formation to join letters in words. They should develop an awareness of the importance of clear and neat presentation, in order to communicate their meaning effectively.	00	00			00				All
■ 3	**Standard English and language study**									
a	Pupils should be introduced to the vocabulary, grammar and structures of written standard English, including subject–verb agreement, and the use of the verb 'to be' in past and present tenses. They should be taught to apply their existing linguistic knowledge, drawn from oral language and their experience of reading, to develop their understanding of the sentence and how word choice and order are crucial to clarity of meaning. Pupils should be given opportunities to discuss the organization of more complex texts, and the way sentences link together.	?	✓		✓	✓			✓	All
b	Pupils' interest in words and their meanings should be developed, and their vocabulary should be extended through consideration and discussion of words with similar meanings, opposites, and words with more than one meaning.	00	✓		✓		00			All

2 MATHEMATICS

The sections of the programme of study interrelate. Developing mathematical language, selecting and using materials, and developing reasoning, should be set in the context of the other areas of mathematics. Sorting, classifying, making comparisons and searching for patterns should apply to work on number, shape and space, and handling data. The use of number should permeate work on measures and handling data.

	Active	Interactive	Decision making	Reflecting	Representing	Play	Outdoor	Equal opportunities	Cross-curricular links
Using and applying mathematics									
■ 1 Pupils should be given opportunities to:									
a use and apply mathematics in practical tasks, in real-life problems and within mathematics itself;	✓	oo	oo	✓		✓	?		oo
b explain their thinking to support the development of their reasoning.	oo	oo	oo	✓					oo
■ 2 Making and monitoring decisions to solve problems									
Pupils should be taught to:									
a select and use the appropriate mathematics;									
b select and use mathematical equipment and materials;	✓	oo	✓			?	?		
c develop different mathematical approaches and look for ways to overcome difficulties;	✓	oo	✓	✓		?	?		
d organize and check their work.			✓	✓					
■ 3 Developing mathematical language and communication									
Pupils should be taught to:									
a understand the language of number, properties of shapes and comparatives, e.g. 'bigger than', 'next to', 'before';	✓	✓	oo	✓		oo	oo		oo
b relate numerals and other mathematical symbols, e.g. '+', '=', to a range of situations;					✓				
c discuss their work, responding to and asking mathematical questions;		✓		✓					
d use a variety of forms of mathematical presentation.				✓	✓	oo			
■ 4 Developing mathematical reasoning									
Pupils should be taught to:									
a recognize simple patterns and relationships and make related predictions about them;									
b ask questions including 'What would happen if?' and 'Why?', e.g. considering the behaviour of a programmable toy;	✓	✓	✓	oo		oo			
c understand general statements, e.g. 'all even numbers divide by 2', and investigate whether particular cases match them.	✓								
Number									
■ 1 Pupils should be given opportunities to:									
a develop flexible methods of working with number, orally and mentally;									
b encounter numbers greater than 1000;									
c use a variety of practical resources and contexts;	✓	oo				?	?		
d use calculators both as a means to explore number and as a tool for calculating with realistic data, e.g. numbers with several digits;	✓								
e record in a variety of ways, including ways that relate to their mental work;	oo		✓	✓	✓				

	Active	Interactive	Decision making	Reflecting	Representing	Play	Outdoor	Equal opportunities	Cross-curricular links
f use computer software, including a database.	✓	00	00						IT
■ 2 Developing an understanding of place value									
Pupils should be taught to:									
a count orally up to 10 and beyond, knowing the number names; count collections of objects, checking the total; count in steps of different sizes, e.g. count on from 5 in steps of 2 or 3; recognize sequences, including odd and even numbers;	00	00			00	00	00		
b read, write and order numbers, initially to 10, progressing up to 1000, developing an understanding that the position of a digit signifies its value; begin to approximate larger numbers to the nearest 10 or 100;	00				00				
c recognize and use in context simple fractions, including halves and quarters, decimal notation in recording money, and negative numbers, e.g. a temperature scale, a number line, a calculator display.	✓	00			00				
■ 3 Understanding relationships between numbers and developing methods of computation									
Pupils should be taught to:									
a use repeating patterns to develop ideas of regularity and sequencing;					00				
b explore and record patterns in addition and subtraction, and then patterns of multiples, e.g. 3, 6, 9, 12, explaining their patterns and using them to make predictions; progress to exploring further patterns involving multiplication and division, including those within a hundred-square of multiplication facts;	✓			✓					
c know addition and subtraction facts to 20, and develop a range of mental methods for finding, from known facts, those that they cannot recall; learn multiplication and division facts relating to the 2s, 5s, 10s, and use these to learn other facts, e.g. double multiples of 2 to produce multiples of 4, and to develop mental methods for finding new results;	✓	00	✓	00					
d develop a variety of methods for adding and subtracting, including using the fact that subtraction is the inverse of addition;	✓		✓	✓	00				
e use a basic calculator, reading the display, e.g. use the constant function to explore repeated addition.	✓								IT
■ 4 Solving numerical problems									
Pupils should be taught to:									
a understand the operations of addition, subtraction as taking away and comparison, and the relationship between them, recognize situations to which they apply and use them to solve problems with whole numbers, including situations involving money;	✓		✓	✓					
b understand the operations of multiplication, and division as sharing and repeated subtraction, and use them to solve problems with whole numbers or money, understanding and dealing appropriately with remainders;	✓		✓	✓					
c choose a suitable method of computation, using apparatus where appropriate, or a calculator where the numbers include several digits;	✓		✓	✓					
d begin to check answers in different ways, e.g. repeating the calculation in a different order or using a different method, and gain a feel for the appropriate size of an answer.			✓	✓					

	Active	Interactive	Decision making	Reflecting	Representing	Play	Outdoor	Equal opportunities	Cross-curricular links
5 Classifying, representing and interpreting data									
Pupils should be taught to:									
a sort and classify a set of objects using criteria related to their properties, e.g. size, shape, mass;	✓	00	✓	✓		00	00		Science
b collect, record and interpret data arising from an area of interest, using an increasing range of charts, diagrams, tables and graphs.	✓			✓					

Shape, space and measures

	Active	Interactive	Decision making	Reflecting	Representing	Play	Outdoor	Equal opportunities	Cross-curricular links
1 Pupils should be given opportunities to:									
a gain a wide range of practical experience using a variety of materials;	✓	00	00			✓	00		
b use IT devices, e.g. programmable toys, turtle graphics packages;	✓	00	00			00	?		00
c use purposeful contexts for measuring.	✓	00	00	00		✓	00		
2 Understanding and using patterns and properties of shape									
Pupils should be taught to:									
a describe and discuss shapes and patterns that can be seen or visualized;	✓	✓		00	✓				
b make common 3-D and 2-D shapes and models, working with increasing care and accuracy; begin to classify shapes according to mathematical criteria;	✓	00	✓	✓		✓	00		Art, design and technology
c recognize and use the geometrical features of shapes, including vertices, sides/edges and surfaces, rectangles (including squares), circles, triangles, cubes, cuboids, progressing to hexagons, pentagons, cylinders and spheres; recognize reflective symmetry in simple cases.	✓	00	✓	00		✓	?		
3 Understanding and using properties of position and movement									
Pupils should be taught to:									
a describe positions, using common words; recognize movements in a straight line, i.e. translations, and rotations, and combine them in simple ways; copy, continue and make patterns;	✓		00			00	00		
b understand angle as a measure of turn and recognize quarter-turns and half-turns, e.g. giving instructions for rotating a programmable toy; recognize right angles.	✓	00	00			00	00		
4 Understanding and using measures									
Pupils should be taught to:									
a compare objects and events using appropriate language, by direct comparison, and then using common non-standard and standard units of length, mass and capacity, e.g. 'three-and-a-bit metres long', 'as heavy as 10 conkers', 'about three beakers full'; begin to use a wider range of standard units, including standard units of time, choosing units appropriate to a situation; estimate with these units;	✓	00	✓	✓	00	00	00		
b choose and use simple measuring instruments, reading and interpreting numbers and scales with some accuracy.	✓	00	✓	✓					

3 SCIENCE

The requirements in this section of the programme of study apply across experimental and investigative science, life processes and living things, materials and their properties, and physical processes.

Science

		Active	Interactive	Decision making	Reflecting	Representing	Play	Outdoor	Equal opportunities	Cross-curricular links
1	**Systematic enquiry**									
	Pupils should be given opportunities to:									
a	ask questions, e.g. 'How?', 'Why?', 'What will happen if . . .?'	✓	✓	✓	✓		00	00		00
b	use focused exploration and investigation to acquire scientific knowledge, understanding and skills;	✓	00		✓		00	00		
c	use both first-hand experience and simple secondary sources to obtain information;	✓	00	00	✓		✓	✓		00
d	use IT to collect, store, retrieve and present scientific information.	✓	00	00	00	✓				✓
2	**Science in everyday life**									
	Pupils should be given opportunities to:									
a	relate their understanding of science to domestic and environmental contexts;		✓		✓		?	?		
b	consider ways in which science is relevant to their personal health;		✓	00	✓					00
c	consider how to treat living things and the environment with care and sensitivity.		00	00	✓			00		
3	**The nature of scientific ideas**									
	Pupils should be given opportunities to:									
a	relate simple scientific ideas to the evidence for them.	✓	00		✓					
4	**Communication**									
	Pupils should be taught to:									
a	use scientific vocabulary to name and describe living things, materials, phenomena and processes;	00	00	00	✓	✓		00		00
b	present scientific information in a number of ways, through drawings, diagrams, tables and charts, and in speech and writing.	00	00	✓	00	✓				
5	**Health and safety**									
	Pupils should be taught to:									
a	recognize hazards and risks when working with living things and materials;	00	00				00	00		
b	follow simple instructions to control the risks to themselves.									

Experimental and investigative science

Contexts derived from life processes and living things, materials and their properties and physical processes should be used to teach pupils about experimental and investigative methods. On some occasions, the whole process of investigating an idea should be carried out by pupils themselves.

		Active	Interactive	Decision making	Reflecting	Representing	Play	Outdoor	Equal opportunities	Cross-curricular links
1	**Planning experimental work**									
	Pupils should be taught:									
a	to turn ideas suggested to them, and their own ideas, into a form that can be investigated;	00	00	✓	✓	✓	00	00		

		Active	Interactive	Decision making	Reflecting	Representing	Play	Outdoor	Equal opportunities	Cross-curricular links
b	that thinking about what is expected to happen can be useful when planning what to do;			✓	✓					
c	to recognize when a test or comparison is unfair.	✓	00	00	✓		00	00		
2	**Obtaining evidence**									
	Pupils should be taught:									
a	to explore using appropriate senses;	✓	✓				✓	00		
b	to make observations and measurements;	✓	00				00	00		
c	to make a record of observations and measurements.	✓	00			✓				
3	**Considering evidence**									
	Pupils should be taught:									
a	to communicate what happened during their work;	✓	✓	00	✓					
b	to use drawings, tables and bar charts to present results;			✓	00	✓				
c	to make simple comparisons;	✓	00	00	✓		00	00		
d	to use results to draw conclusions;				✓					
e	to indicate whether the evidence collected supports any prediction made;		✓	✓	✓					
f	to try to explain what they found out, drawing on their knowledge and understanding.		✓		✓					

Life processes and living things

Work on life processes should be related to pupils' knowledge of animals and plants in the local environment.

		Active	Interactive	Decision making	Reflecting	Representing	Play	Outdoor	Equal opportunities	Cross-curricular links
1	**Life processes**									
	Pupils should be taught:									
a	the differences between things that are living and things that have never been alive;	00			00					
b	that animals, including humans, move, feed, grow, use their senses and reproduce.	00	✓		00					
2	**Humans as organisms**									
	Pupils should be taught:									
a	to name the main external parts, e.g. hand, elbow, knee, of the human body;	✓								00
b	that humans need food and water to stay alive;	00								
c	that taking exercise and eating the right types and amount of food help humans to keep healthy;	00		00	00					
d	about the role of drugs as medicines;			✓	00					
e	that humans can produce babies and these babies grow into children and adults;				00				00	
f	that humans have senses which enable them to be aware of the world around them.	✓	00		00			00		

		Active	Interactive	Decision making	Reflecting	Representing	Play	Outdoor	Equal opportunities	Cross-curricular links
■ 3	**Green plants as organisms**									
	Pupils should be taught:									
a	that plants need light and water to grow									
b	to recognize and name the leaf, flower, stem and root of flowering plants;	✓				✓			00	
c	that flowering plants grow and produce seeds which, in turn, produce new plants.	00			✓			00		
■ 4	**Variation and classification**									
	Pupils should be taught:									
a	to recognize similarities and differences between themselves and other pupils;	✓	✓		✓		00	00	00	
b	that living things can be grouped according to observable similarities and differences.	✓	00	✓	✓			00		
■ 5	**Living things in their environment**									
	Pupils should be taught:									
a	that there are different kinds of plants and animals in the local environment;				00			✓		
b	that there are differences between local environments and that these affect which animals and plants are found there.				00			✓		

Materials and their properties

Work on everyday uses of materials should be related to pupils' knowledge of the properties of the materials and of objects made from them, and to their knowledge of the way changes affect the materials.

		Active	Interactive	Decision making	Reflecting	Representing	Play	Outdoor	Equal opportunities	Cross-curricular links
■ 1	**Grouping materials**									
	Pupils should be taught:									
a	to use their senses to explore and recognize the similarities and differences between materials;	✓	00	00	✓		00	00		
b	to sort materials into groups on the basis of simple properties, including texture, appearance, transparency and whether they are magnetic or non-magnetic;	✓	00	✓	✓		00	00		
c	to recognize and name common types of material, e.g. metal, plastic, wood, paper, rock, and to know that some of these materials are found naturally;	✓	00	00	00		?	?		
d	that many materials, e.g. glass, wood, wool, have a variety of uses;	?	?		00		?	?		
e	that materials are chosen for specific uses, e.g. glass for windows, wool for clothing, on the basis of their properties.	?	?	00	✓					
■ 2	**Changing materials**									
	Pupils should be taught:									
a	that objects made from some materials can be changed in shape by processes including squashing, bending, twisting and stretching;	✓	00				✓	00		
b	to describe the way some everyday materials, e.g. water, chocolate, bread, clay, change when they are heated or cooled.	✓	00		00		00			

	Active	Interactive	Decision making	Reflecting	Representing	Play	Outdoor	Equal opportunities	Cross-curricular links
Physical processes Work on observable effects should be related to pupils' knowledge of physical phenomena.									
1 Electricity Pupils should be taught:									
a that many everyday appliances use electricity;	✓	00							
b to construct simple circuits involving batteries, wires, bulbs and buzzers;	✓	00	00	00		00			00
c that electrical devices will not work if there is a break in the circuit.	✓	00		✓		00			00
2 Forces and motion Pupils should be taught:									
a to describe the movement of familiar things, e.g. cars getting faster, slowing down, changing direction;	✓	00	00	✓		✓	00		
b that both pushes and pulls are examples of forces;	✓	00		✓		✓	00		
c that forces can make things speed up, slow down or change direction;	✓	00	00	✓		✓	00		
d that forces can change the shapes of objects.	✓	00	00	✓		✓	00		
3 Light and sound Pupils should be taught:									
Light and dark									
a that light comes from a variety of sources, including the Sun;	✓		00	00		00	✓		
b that darkness is the absence of light;									
Making and detecting sounds									
c that there are many kinds of sound and many sources of sound;	✓	00	00	00		00	00		
d that sounds travel away from sources, getting fainter as they do so;	✓	00	00	00		00	00		
e that sounds are heard when they enter the ear.	✓								

4 DESIGN AND TECHNOLOGY

Pupils should be taught to develop their design and technology capability through combining their designing and making skills (paragraphs 3 and 4) with knowledge and understanding (paragraph 5) in order to design and make products.

		Active	Interactive	Decision making	Reflecting	Representing	Play	Outdoor	Equal opportunities	Cross-curricular links
■ 1	**Pupils should develop their design and technology capability through:**									
a	assignments in which they design and make products;	✓	00	✓	00	00	00	00	!	00
b	focused practical tasks in which they develop and practise particular skills and knowledge;	✓	00	00			00	00	!	00
c	activities in which they investigate, disassemble and evaluate simple products.	✓	00	00	✓		00	00	!	
■ 2	**Pupils should be given opportunities to:**									
a	work with a range of materials and components, including sheet materials, items that can be assembled to make products, e.g. reclaimed material, textiles, food and construction kits;	✓	00	00		00	00	00	!	00
b	investigate how the working characteristics of materials can be changed to suit different purposes;	✓	00	✓	00	00	00	00	!	
c	apply skills, knowledge and understanding from the programmes of study of other subjects, where appropriate, including art, mathematics and science.	00	00	✓	✓				!	✓
■ 3	**Designing skills**									
	Pupils should be taught to:									
a	draw on their own experience to help generate ideas;			✓	✓	✓			!	
b	clarify their ideas through discussion;		✓	00	00				!	
c	develop their ideas through shaping, assembling and rearranging materials and components;	✓	00	✓	✓	✓	00	00	!	00
d	develop and communicate their design ideas by making freehand drawings, and by modelling their ideas in other ways, e.g. by using actual materials and components with temporary fixings;	✓	00	✓	✓		00		!	00
e	make suggestions about how to proceed;	00	✓	✓	✓		00		!	
f	consider their design ideas as these develop, and identify strengths and weaknesses.		00	✓	✓				!	
■ 4	**Making skills**									
	Pupils should be taught to:									
a	select materials, tools and techniques;	✓	00	✓	00				!	
b	measure, mark out, cut and shape a range of materials;	✓	00	00					!	00
c	assemble, join and combine materials and components;	✓	00	00		✓	00		!	
d	apply simple finishing techniques, e.g. painting;	✓	00	00		00			!	
e	make suggestions about how to proceed;		✓	✓	✓				!	
f	evaluate their products as these are developed, identifying strengths and weaknesses.			✓	✓				!	

	Active	Interactive	Decision making	Reflecting	Representing	Play	Outdoor	Equal opportunities	Cross-curricular links
■ 5 **Knowledge and understanding**									
Pupils should be taught:									
a to use simple mechanisms, including wheels and axles, and joints that allow movement;	✓	00				00	00	!	
b how to make their structures more stable and withstand greater loads;	00	00	00	00		00	00	!	00
c to investigate and disassemble simple products in order to learn how they function;	✓	00	00	00		00	00	!	
d to relate the ways things work to their intended purpose, how materials and components have been used, people's needs, and what users say about them;	?	?	00	✓		00		!	
e that the quality of a product depends on how well it is made and how well it meets its purpose;	?	?		00				!	
f simple knowledge and understanding of health and safety, as consumers and when working with materials and components, including:			✓	00				!	
■ considering the hazards and risks in their activities;				00				!	
■ following simple instructions to control risk to themselves;								!	
g to use the appropriate vocabulary for naming and describing the equipment, materials and components they use.		✓						!	

5 INFORMATION TECHNOLOGY

Pupils should be taught to use IT equipment and software confidently and purposefully to communicate and handle information, and to support their problem solving, recording and expressive work.

	Active	Interactive	Decision making	Reflecting	Representing	Play	Outdoor	Equal opportunities	Cross-curricular links
1 Pupils should be given opportunities to:									
a use a variety of IT equipment and software, including microcomputers and various keyboards, to carry out a variety of functions in a range of contexts;	✓	OO	OO			?	?		
b explore the use of computer systems and control technology in everyday life;	✓	OO		OO		?	?		
c examine and discuss their experiences of IT, and look at the use of IT in the outside world.	✓	✓	✓	✓					OO
2 Communicating and handling information									
Pupils should be taught to:									
a generate and communicate their ideas in different forms, using text, tables, pictures and sound;	✓	✓	OO	✓					✓
b enter and store information;	✓								
c retrieve, process and display information that has been stored.	✓			OO					
3 Controlling and modelling									
Pupils should be taught to:									
a recognize that control is integral to many everyday devices;	✓			OO					
b give direct signals or commands that produce a variety of outcomes, and describe the effects of their actions;	✓	OO	✓			?	?		
c use IT-based models or simulations to explore aspects of real and imaginary situations.	✓	OO		OO		✓			

6 HISTORY

Pupils should be given opportunities to develop an awareness of the past and of the ways in which it was different from the present. They should be helped to set their study of the past in a chronological framework and to understand some of the ways in which we find out about the past. The areas of study and the key elements, outlined below, should be taught together.

	Active	Interactive	Decision making	Reflecting	Representing	Play	Outdoor	Equal opportunities	Cross-curricular links
Areas of study									
■ 1 Pupils should be taught about the everyday life, work, leisure and culture of men, women and children in the past, e.g. clothes, diet, everyday objects, houses, shops and other buildings, jobs, transport, entertainment. In progressing from familiar situations to those more distant in time and place, pupils should be given opportunities to investigate:	00	00		00			00	00	
a changes in their own lives and those of their family or adults around them;	✓	00		00				✓	
b aspects of the way of life of people in Britain in the past beyond living memory.	✓			00				!	
■ 2 Pupils should be taught about the lives of different kinds of famous men and women, including personalities drawn from British history, e.g. rulers, saints, artists, engineers, explorers, inventors, pioneers.								!	
■ 3 Pupils should be taught about past events of different types, including events from the history of Britain, e.g. notable local and national events, events in other countries, events that have been remembered and commemorated by succeeding generations, such as centenaries, religious festivals, anniversaries, the Gunpowder Plot, the Olympic Games.								!	
Key elements									
The key elements are closely related and should be developed through the areas of study, as appropriate. Not all the key elements need to be developed in each area of study.									
■ 1 **Chronology** Pupils should be taught:									
a to sequence events and objects, in order to develop a sense of chronology;	✓		00	00					
b to use common words and phrases relating to the passing of time, e.g. old, new, before, after, long ago, days of the week, months, years.			00			00			
■ 2 **Range and depth of historical knowledge and understanding** Pupils should be taught:									
a about aspects of the past through stories from different periods and cultures, including stories and eyewitness accounts of historical events;				00		00			
b to recognize why people did things, why events happened and what happened as a result;				00					
c to identify differences between ways of life at different times.				00					
■ 3 **Interpretations of history** Pupils should be taught:									
a to identify different ways in which the past is represented, e.g. pictures, written accounts, films, television programmes, plays, songs, reproductions of objects, museum displays.				00	00				

	Active	Interactive	Decision making	Reflecting	Representing	Play	Outdoor	Equal opportunities	Cross-curricular links
■ 4 Historical enquiry									
Pupils should be taught:									
a how to find out about aspects of the past from a range of sources of information, including artefacts, pictures and photographs, adults talking about their own past, written sources, and buildings and sites;			00	00					
b to ask and answer questions about the past.		✓							
■ 5 Organization and communication									
Pupils should be taught:									
a to communicate their awareness and understanding of history in a variety of ways.			00		✓				

7 GEOGRAPHY

		Active	Interactive	Decision making	Reflecting	Representing	Play	Outdoor	Equal opportunities	Cross-curricular links
■ 1	Pupils should be given opportunities to:									
a	investigate the physical and human features of their surroundings;	✓	00				00	✓		00
b	undertake studies that focus on geographical questions, e.g. 'What/Where is it?', 'What is it like?', 'How did it get like this?', and that are based on direct experience, practical activities and fieldwork in the locality of the school; studies should involve the development of skills, and the development of knowledge and understanding about places and themes;	✓	00		✓	00	00	✓		00
c	become aware that the world extends beyond their own locality, both within and outside the United Kingdom, and that the places they study exist within this broader geographical context, e.g. within a town, a region, a country.	?	?		?		?		✓	

Geographical skills

		Active	Interactive	Decision making	Reflecting	Representing	Play	Outdoor	Equal opportunities	Cross-curricular links
■ 2	In investigating places and a theme, pupils should be given opportunities to observe, question and record, and to communicate ideas and information.	✓	✓		✓	✓			✓	
■ 3	Pupils should be taught to:									
a	use geographical terms, e.g. hill, river, road, in exploring their surroundings;	✓					?	✓		
b	undertake fieldwork activities in the locality of the school, e.g. observing housing types, mapping the school playground;	✓				✓		✓		
c	follow directions, including the terms up, down, on, under, behind, in front of, near, far, left, right, north, south, east, west;	✓				00		00		00
d	make maps and plans of real and imaginary places, using pictures and symbols, e.g. a pictorial map of a place featured in a story, a plan of their route from home to school;	✓				✓	00	00	✓	
e	use globes, maps and plans at a variety of scales; the work should include identifying major geographical features, e.g. seas, rivers, cities, locating and naming on a map the constituent countries of the United Kingdom, marking on a map approximately where they live, and following a route;	?			00	00			✓	
f	use secondary sources, e.g. pictures, photographs (including aerial photographs), books, videos, CD-ROM encyclopaedia, to obtain geographical information.	✓		?			?	?	00	

Places

		Active	Interactive	Decision making	Reflecting	Representing	Play	Outdoor	Equal opportunities	Cross-curricular links
■ 4	Two localities should be studied: the locality of the school and a locality, either in the United Kingdom or overseas, in which the physical and/or human features contrast with those in the locality of the school. The locality of the school is its immediate vicinity; it includes the school buildings and grounds and the surrounding area within easy access. The contrasting locality should be an area of similar size.	✓			00				00	00
■ 5	In these studies, pupils should be taught:									
a	about the main physical and human features, e.g. rivers, hills, factories, shops, that give the localities their character;					00	00	00	00	00
b	how localities may be similar and how they may differ, e.g. both areas may have farmland, but animals may be kept on the farms in one area, while in the other crops may be grown;			00	00					

		Active	Interactive	Decision making	Reflecting	Representing	Play	Outdoor	Equal opportunities	Cross-curricular links
c	about the effects of weather on people and their surroundings, e.g. effect of seasonal variations in temperature on clothes people wear;	00		00	00		00	00	00	00
d	how land and buildings, e.g. farms, parks, factories, houses, are used.	?					?	?		00

Thematic study

■ 6 The quality of the environment in any locality, either in the United Kingdom or overseas, should be investigated. In this study, pupils should be taught:

		Active	Interactive	Decision making	Reflecting	Representing	Play	Outdoor	Equal opportunities	Cross-curricular links
a	to express views on the attractive and unattractive features, e.g. tidiness, noise, of the environment concerned, e.g. a play area, a street, a small area of woodland;	✓	✓	✓	✓	?		✓		
b	how that environment is changing, e.g. increasing traffic;	00							00	
c	how the quality of that environment can be sustained and improved, e.g. creating cycle lanes, excluding cars from an area.	00		00	00				00	00

8 PHYSICAL EDUCATION

In each year of the key stage, pupils should be taught three areas of activity: games, gymnastic activities and dance, using indoor and outdoor environments where appropriate. In addition, schools may choose to teach swimming in Key Stage 1 using the programme of study set out in Key Stage 2. Throughout the key stage, pupils should be taught about the changes that occur to their bodies as they exercise, and to recognize the short-term effects of exercise on the body.

Physical education general requirements

Physical education should involve pupils in the continuous process of planning, performing and evaluating. This applies to all areas of activity. The greatest emphasis should be placed on the actual performance aspect of the subject. The following requirements apply to the teaching of physical education across all key stages.

		Active	Interactive	Decision making	Reflecting	Representing	Play	Outdoor	Equal opportunities	Cross-curricular links
■ 1	To promote physical activity and healthy lifestyles, pupils should be taught:									
a	to be physically active;	✓	00				00	00		
b	to adopt the best possible posture and the appropriate use of the body;	00		00						
c	to engage in activities that develop cardiovascular health, flexibility, muscular strength and endurance;	✓	00					00		
d	the increasing need for personal hygiene in relation to vigorous physical activity.								!	
■ 2	To develop positive attitudes, pupils should be taught:									
a	to observe the conventions of fair play, honest competition and good sporting behaviour as individual participants, team members and spectators;	✓	00	00	00			00		
b	how to cope with success and limitations in performance;	✓								
c	to try hard to consolidate their performances;	✓								
d	to be mindful of others and the environment.		00	✓	✓	✓		00		
■ 3	To ensure safe practice, pupils should be taught:									
a	to respond readily to instructions;									
b	to recognize and follow relevant rules, laws, codes, etiquette and safety procedures for different activities or events, in practice and during competition;	00						00		
c	about the safety risks of wearing inappropriate clothing, footwear and jewellery, and why particular clothing, footwear and protection are worn for different activities;								!	
d	how to lift, carry, place and use equipment safely;	✓	00	00	00			00	!	
e	to warm up for and recover from exercise.	✓								

Areas of activity

■ 1 Games

		Active	Interactive	Decision making	Reflecting	Representing	Play	Outdoor	Equal opportunities	Cross-curricular links
	Pupils should be taught:									
a	simple competitive games, including how to play them as individuals and, when ready, in pairs and in small groups;	✓	00	00	00		00	00		
b	to develop and practise a variety of ways of sending (including throwing, striking, rolling and bouncing), receiving and travelling with a ball and other similar games equipment;	✓	00	00				00		

	Active	Interactive	Decision making	Reflecting	Representing	Play	Outdoor	Equal opportunities	Cross-curricular links
c elements of games play that include running, chasing, dodging, avoiding, and awareness of space and other players.	✓	00	00	00			00		
■ 2 **Gymnastic activities**									
Pupils should be taught:									
a different ways of performing the basic actions of travelling using hands and feet, turning, rolling, jumping, balancing, swinging and climbing, both on the floor and using apparatus;	✓						00		
b to link a series of actions both on the floor and using apparatus, and how to repeat them.	✓		00	00			00		
■ 3 **Dance**									
Pupils should be taught:									
a to develop control, coordination, balance, poise and elevation in the basic actions of travelling, jumping, turning, gesture and stillness;	✓								
b to perform movements or patterns, including some from existing dance traditions;	✓	00					00	00	00
c to explore moods and feelings and to develop their response to music through dances, by using rhythmic responses and contrasts of speed, shape, direction and level.	✓	00	00	00	00				

9 MUSIC

Pupils' understanding and enjoyment of music should be developed through activities that bring together requirements from both performing and composing, and listening and appraising wherever possible.

	Active	Interactive	Decision making	Reflecting	Representing	Play	Outdoor	Equal opportunities	Cross-curricular links
1 Pupils should be given opportunities to:									
a use sounds and respond to music individually, in pairs, in groups and as a class;	✓	✓	oo		✓	oo			
b make appropriate use of IT to record sounds.	✓	oo	oo		oo				✓
2 When performing, composing, listening and appraising, pupils should be taught to listen with concentration, exploring, internalizing, e.g. hearing in their heads, and recognizing the musical elements of:				✓					
a pitch (high/low);	✓	oo	✓	✓	oo	✓			
b duration (long/short; pulse or beat; rhythm);	✓	oo	✓	✓	oo	✓			oo
c dynamics (loud/quiet/silence);	✓	oo	✓	✓	oo	✓	oo		
d tempo (fast/slow);	✓	oo	✓	✓	oo	✓	oo		oo
e timbre (quality of sound, e.g. tinkling, rattling, smooth, ringing);	✓	oo	✓	✓	oo	✓	oo		oo
f texture (several sounds played or sung at the same time/one sound on its own);	✓	oo	✓	✓	oo	✓	oo		
and the use of the above within:									
g structure (different sections, e.g. beginning, middle, end; repetition, e.g. repeated patterns, melody, rhythm).	✓	oo	✓	✓	oo	oo			
3 The repertoire chosen for performing and listening should extend pupils' musical experience and knowledge, and develop their appreciation of the richness of our diverse cultural heritage. It should include music in a variety of styles:									
a from different times and cultures;	✓	✓		✓	✓			✓	oo
b by well-known composers and performers, past and present.	✓	✓		✓	✓			✓	oo

Performing and composing

	Active	Interactive	Decision making	Reflecting	Representing	Play	Outdoor	Equal opportunities	Cross-curricular links
4 Pupils should be given opportunities to:									
a control sounds made by the voice and a range of tuned and untuned instruments;	✓	oo	oo		oo	oo	oo		
b perform with others, and develop awareness of audience, venue and occasion;	✓	✓		✓		oo	oo		
c compose in response to a variety of stimuli, and explore a range of resources, e.g. voices, instruments, sounds from the environment;	✓	oo	oo	✓	✓	oo	oo		
d communicate musical ideas to others;	✓	✓	oo	oo	✓	oo	oo		oo
e listen to, and develop understanding of, music from different times and places, applying knowledge to their own work;	✓	oo	oo	✓				✓	
f respond to, and evaluate, live performances and recorded music, including their own and others' compositions and performances.	✓	✓		✓					
5 Pupils should be taught to:									
a sing songs from memory, developing control of breathing, dynamics, rhythm and pitch;	✓								
b play simple pieces and accompaniments, and perform short musical patterns by ear and from symbols;	✓	oo							

		Active	Interactive	Decision making	Reflecting	Representing	Play	Outdoor	Equal opportunities	Cross-curricular links
c	sing unison songs and play pieces, developing awareness of other performers;	✓	✓							
d	rehearse and share their music making;	✓	✓				00	00		
e	improvise musical patterns, e.g. invent and change patterns whilst playing and singing;	✓					✓	00		
f	explore, create, select and organize sounds in simple structures;	✓		✓	✓		✓	00		
g	use sounds to create musical effects, e.g. to suggest a machine or a walk through a forest;	✓	00	✓	✓	✓	✓	00		
h	record their compositions using symbols, where appropriate.	✓				✓				

Listening and appraising

■ 6 Pupils should be taught to:

		Active	Interactive	Decision making	Reflecting	Representing	Play	Outdoor	Equal opportunities	Cross-curricular links
a	recognize how sounds can be made in different ways, e.g. by blowing, plucking, shaking, vocalizing;	00	00			✓	00	00		
b	recognize how sounds are used in music to achieve particular effects, e.g. to soothe, to excite;				✓					
c	recognize that music comes from different times and places;			00	✓					00
d	respond to musical elements, and the changing character and mood of a piece of music by means of dance or other suitable forms of expression;	✓	00		✓	✓	00	00		
e	describe in simple terms the sounds they have made, listened to, performed, composed or heard, including everyday sounds.	✓	00	00	00	✓				

10 ART

Art should be interpreted as 'art, craft and design' throughout. Pupils' understanding and enjoyment of art, craft and design should be developed through activities that bring together requirements from both investigating and making, and knowledge and understanding, wherever possible.

	Active	Interactive	Decision making	Reflecting	Representing	Play	Outdoor	Equal opportunities	Cross-curricular links
■ 1 Pupils should be given opportunities to experience different approaches to art, craft and design, including those that involve working individually, in groups and as a whole class.	✓	✓	00	00	✓	00	00		00
■ 2 In order to develop visual perception, pupils should be taught the creative, imaginative and practical skills needed to:									
a express ideas and feelings;	✓				✓	00			
b record observations;	✓		00	✓					
c design and make images and artefacts.	✓		✓		✓	00			00
■ 3 In order to develop visual literacy, pupils should be taught about the different ways in which ideas, feelings and meanings are communicated in visual form.									
■ 4 Throughout their work, pupils should be taught about visual and, where appropriate, tactile elements, including:									
a pattern and texture in natural and made forms;	00		00	00	00				00
b colour matching and how colour is mixed from primary colours;	00		00	?		00	00		00
c how images are made using line and tone;	00		00	?		00	00		
d the use of shape, form and space in images and artefacts.	00		00	?		00	00		00
■ 5 Pupils should be introduced to the work of artists, craftspeople and designers, e.g. drawing, painting, printmaking, photography, sculpture, ceramics, textiles, graphic design, architecture, in order to develop their appreciation of the richness of our diverse cultural heritage. The selection should include work in a variety of genres and styles from:									
a the locality;				00				✓	
b the past and present;				00				✓	00
c a variety of cultures, Western and non-Western.				00				✓	00
■ 6 Pupils should be taught to use materials, tools and techniques for practical work safely and in accordance with health and safety requirements.	✓		✓	✓					00

Investigating and making

	Active	Interactive	Decision making	Reflecting	Representing	Play	Outdoor	Equal opportunities	Cross-curricular links
■ 7 Pupils should be given opportunities to:									
a record responses, including observations of the natural and made environment;	00		✓	✓			✓		00
b gather resources and materials, using them to stimulate and develop ideas;	✓		✓						
c explore and use two- and three-dimensional media, working on a variety of scales;	✓		✓	00					00
d review and modify their work as it progresses;			✓	✓					
e develop understanding of the work of artists, craftspeople and designers, applying knowledge to their own work;				00				✓	
f respond to and evaluate art, craft and design, including their own and others' work.			✓	✓				✓	

		Active	Interactive	Decision making	Reflecting	Representing	Play	Outdoor	Equal opportunities	Cross-curricular links
■ 8	Pupils should be taught to:									
a	record what has been experienced, observed and imagined;	✓				✓			✓	
b	recognize images and artefacts as sources of ideas for their work;				00					
c	select and sort images and artefacts, and use this source material as a basis for their work;			✓	00				✓	
d	experiment with tools and techniques for drawing, painting, printmaking, collage and sculpture, exploring a range of materials, including textiles;	✓		✓		✓			✓	
e	experiment with visual elements, e.g. pattern, texture, colour, line, tone, shape, form, space, to make images and artefacts, using the range of media in 8d;	✓		✓	✓					
f	review what they have done and describe what they might change or develop in future work.		✓	✓	✓	✓				

Knowledge and understanding

		Active	Interactive	Decision making	Reflecting	Representing	Play	Outdoor	Equal opportunities	Cross-curricular links
■ 9	Pupils should be taught to:									
a	identify in the school and the locality the work of artists, craftspeople and designers;	✓							✓	
b	recognize visual elements, e.g. pattern, texture, colour, line, tone, shape, form, space, in images and artefacts;			✓						
c	recognize differences and similarities in art, craft and design from different times and places;			✓	✓				✓	
d	respond to the ideas, methods or approaches used in different styles and traditions;			✓					✓	
e	describe works of art, craft and design in simple terms, and explain what they think and feel about these.		✓	✓	00					

REFERENCES

Abbott, L. (1994) 'Play is ace!' Developing play in schools and classrooms, in J. Moyles (ed.) *The Excellence of Play*. Buckingham: Open University Press.

Alexander, R. (1994) *What Primary Curriculum: Dearing and Beyond*, paper presented to an Association for Science Education conference, Sutton Coldfield, 11 June.

Alexander, R., Rose, J. and Woodhead, C. (1992) *Curriculum Organisation and Classroom Practice in Primary Schools: A Discussion Paper*. London: DES.

Anning, A. (1995) *A National Curriculum for the Early Years*. Buckingham: Open University Press.

Athey, C. (1990) *Extending Thought in Young Children*. London: Paul Chapman.

Ball, C. (1995) *Start Right: The Importance of Early Learning*. London: Royal Society of Arts.

Bennett, N. and Kell, J. (1989) *A Good Start? Four Year Olds in Infant Schools*. Oxford: Blackwell.

Bennett, N., Wood, L. and Rogers, S. (1997) *Teaching through Play: Teachers' Theories and Classroom Practice*. Buckingham: Open University Press.

Blatchford, P. (1989) *Playtime in the Primary School: Problems and Improvements*. Slough: NFER Nelson.

Blenkin, G.M. and Kelly. A.V. (eds) (1996) *The National Curriculum and Early Learning: An Evaluation*. London: Paul Chapman.

Board of Education (1933) *Report of the Consultative Committee on Infant and Nursery School* [The Hadow Report]. London: HMSO.

Brown, G. and Wragg, E. (1993) *Questioning*. London: Routledge.

Browne, N. and France, P. (eds) (1986) *Untying the Apron Strings*. Milton Keynes: Open University Press.

Bruce, T. (1987) *Early Childhood Education*. London: Hodder and Stoughton.

Bruce, T. (1991) *Time to Play in Early Childhood Education*. London: Hodder and Stoughton.

Bruce, T. (1996) *Helping Young Children to Play*. London: Hodder and Stoughton.

Bruner, J. (1977) *The Process of Instruction*. Cambridge, MA: Harvard University Press.

Chang, D.L. and Wells, G. (1988). The literate potential of collaborative talk, in M. MacLure, T. Philips and A.

Wilkinson (eds) *Oracy Matters*. Milton Keynes: Open University Press.

Claxton, G. (1997) *Hare Brain, Tortoise Mind*. London: Fourth Estate.

David, T., Curtis, A. and Siraj-Blatchford I. (1993) *Effective Teaching in the Early Years: Fostering Children's Learning in Nursery and Infant Classes*. London: OMEP.

Department of Education and Science [DES] (1989) *The National Curriculum*. London: HMSO.

Department for Education and Employment [DfEE] (1995) *The National Curriculum*. London: HMSO.

Dowling, M. (1995) *Starting School at Four: A Joint Endeavour*. London: Paul Chapman.

Dunn, J. (1988) *The Beginnings of Social Understanding*. Cambridge, MA: Harvard University Press.

Dunne, E. and Bennett, N. (1990) *Talking and Learning in Groups*. Basingstoke: Macmillan.

Early Childhood Education Forum (forthcoming) *Quality in Diversity*. London: National Children's Bureau.

Early Years Curriculum Group [EYCG] (1989) *Early Childhood Education: The Early Years Curriculum and the National Curriculum*. Stoke-on-Trent: Trentham Books.

Early Years Curriculum Group (1992) *First Things First, Educating Young Children: A Guide for Parents and Governors*. Oldham: Madeleine Lindley.

Edgington, M. (1998) *The Nursery Teacher in Action: Teaching Three, Four and Five Year Olds*. London: Paul Chapman.

Egan, K. (1988) *Primary Understanding*. London: Routledge.

Engel, D.M. and Whitehead, M.R. (1996) Which English? Standard English and language variety: some educational perspectives, *English in Education*, 30(1) Spring: 36–49.

Equal Opportunities Commission and Office for Standards in Education (1996) *The Gender Divide: Performance Differences between Boys and Girls at School*. London: HMSO.

Field, C. and Lally, M. (1996) *Planning for Progress*. London: Tower Hamlets LEA.

Fisher, J. (1996) *Starting from the Child?* Buckingham: Open University Press.

Galton, M. and Williamson, J. (1992) *Groupwork and the Primary Classroom*. London: Routledge.

Gardner, H. (1993) *The Unschooled Mind*. New York and Glasgow: Fontana Press.

Gura, P. (ed.) (1992) *Exploring Learning: Young Children and Blockplay*. London: Paul Chapman.

Hall, N. and Abbot, L. (eds) (1991) *Play in the Primary Curriculum*. London: Hodder and Stoughton.

Hall, N. and Robinson, A. (1995) *Exploring Writing as Play in the Early Years*. London: David Fulton.

Harris, J. (1994) *What Primary Curriculum: Dearing and Beyond*, paper presented to an Association for Science Education conference, Birmingham, 11 June.

Hastings, N. and Schwieso, J. (1995) Tasks and tables: the effects of seating arrangements on task engagement, *Primary Schools Education Research*, 37(3): 279–91.

Hohmann, M. and Weikart, D. (1995) *Educating Young Children*. Ypsilanti, MI: High/Scope Press.

Holt, J. (1989) *Learning all the Time*. Ticknell: Education Now Publishing Co-operative.

Hughes, M. (1986) *Children and Number*. Oxford: Blackwell.

Katz, L. and Chard, S. (1989) *Engaging Children's Minds: The Topic Approach*. New York: Ablex.

Katz, L. and MacLellan, D. (1991) *The Teacher's Role in the Social Development of Young Children*. Urbana, IL: Eric Clearing House on Elementary and Early Childhood Education.

Laevers, F. (1994) The innovative project – experiential education and the definition of quality in education, in F. Laevers (ed.) *Defining and Assessing Quality in Early Childhood Education*. Studia Paedogogica, No. 16. Leuven, Belgium: Leuven University Press.

Lally, M. (1995) Principles to practice in early years education, in R. Campbell and L. Miller (eds) *Supporting Children in the Early Years*. Stoke-on-Trent: Trentham Books.

Lindqvist, G. (1995) *The Aesthetics of Play: A Didactic Study of Play and Culture in Pre-schools*. Acta Universitatis Upsaliensis, Uppsala Studies in Education 62, Stockholm: Almqvist and Wiksell International.

Matthews, J. (1994) *Helping Children to Draw and Paint in Early Childhood*. London: Hodder and Stoughton.

Maude, P. (1996) 'How do I do this better?' From movement development into early years physical education, in D. Whitebread (ed.) *Teaching and Learning in the Early Years*. London: Routledge.

McMillan, M. (1930) *The Nursery School*. London: Dent.

McNeish, D. and Roberts, H. (1995) *Playing it Safe: Today's Children at Play*. Ilford: Barnardo's.

Mithen, S. (1996) *The Prehistory of the Mind*. London: Thames and Hudson.

Moss, P. and Penn, H. (1996) *Transforming Nursery Education*. London: Paul Chapman.

Moyles, J. (1989) *Just Playing? The Role and Status of Play in Early Education*. Milton Keynes: Open University Press.

Moyles, J. (1991) *Play as a Learning Process in Your Classroom*. London: Mary Glasgow.

Moyles, J. (1992) *Organizing for Learning in the Primary Classroom*. Buckingham: Open University Press.

Moyles, J. with Suschitzky, W. (1997) *Jills of All Trades? Classroom Assistants in Key Stage 1 Classes*. Leicester: University of Leicester for the Association of Teachers and Lecturers.

Nutbrown, C. (ed.) (1996) *Respectful Educators – Capable Learners: Children's Rights and Early Education*. London: Paul Chapman.

Odam, G. (1995) *The Sounding Symbol*. Cheltenham: Stanley Thornes.

Office for Standards in Education [Ofsted] (1993) *First Class. HMI Report on Reception Class Provision*. London: HMSO.

Office for Standards in Education (1994) *Early Years Training Material for Additional Inspectors*. London: Ofsted.

Papousek, H., Jurgens, U. and Papousek, M. (eds) (1992) *Non-verbal Vocal Communication: Comparative and Developmental Aspects*. New York: Cambridge University Press.

Roberts, R. (1995) *Self Esteem and Successful Early Learning*. London: Hodder and Stoughton.

Rowlands, S. (1984) *The Enquiring Classroom: An Introduction to Children's Learning*. Lewes: Falmer Press.

Rubin, K., Fein, G. and Vandenburg, B. (1983) Play, in E.M. Hetherington (ed.) *Manual of Child Psychology: Socialization, Personality and Social Development* (Vol. IV). New York: Wiley.

Runnymede Trust (1993) *Equality Assurance in Schools*. Stoke-on-Trent: Trentham Books.

SCAA (1995) *Planning the Curriculum at Key Stages 1 and 2*. London: Department for Education and Employment.

SCAA (1996) *Desirable Outcomes for Children's Learning on Entering Compulsory Education*. London: Department for Education and Employment.

SCAA (1997) *The National Framework for Baseline Assessment*. London: Department for Education and Employment.

Sotto, E. (1994) *When Teaching Becomes Learning*. London: Cassell.

Titman, W. (1991) *Special People, Special Places*. London: World Wildlife Trust and Learning through Landscapes.

Tizard, B., Blatchford, P., Burke, J., Farquhar, C. and Plewis, I. (1988) *Young Children at School in the Inner City*. Hove: Lawrence Erlbaum Associates.

Tymms, P. (1991) *Baseline Assessment and Value Added. A Report to SCAA*. CEM Centre, University of Durham.

Vygotsky, L. (1978) *Mind in Society*. Cambridge, MA: Harvard University Press.

Warham, S. (1993) *Primary Teaching and the Negotiation of Power*. London: Paul Chapman.

Wells, G. (1987) *The Meaning Makers: Children Learning Language and Using Language to Learn*. London: Hodder and Stoughton.

Whalley, M. (1995) *Learning to be Strong*. London: Hodder and Stoughton.

Wood, D. (1988) *How Children Think and Learn*. Oxford: Blackwell.